BECOMING JEZEBEL

Copyright 2023 John Burns

All rights reserved.

ISBN: 979-8-3893150-0-6

All rights reserved. Non-commercial interests may reproduce portions of this book without the express written permission of the author, provided the text does not exceed 500 words. When reproducing text from this book, include the following credit line: "Becoming Jezebel by John Burns. Used by permission."

Commercial interests: No part of this publication may be reproduced in any form, stored in a retrieval system, or transmitted in any form by any means - electronic, photocopy, recording, or otherwise - without prior written permission of the publisher, except as provided by the United States of America copyright law.

BECOMING JEZEBEL

John Burns

Dedication

To the men of Task Force Ranger and Bravo Company 3/75 Ranger Regiment.

To Jesus Christ for saving me from myself.

Table of Contents

Dedication 4
Preface 7
Mercy 13
   The Time of Jezebel 15
   EthBaal King of Tyre 20
   Jereboam I 25
   North South Conundrum 30
   From Jezebel to Planned Parenthood 35
   For this Reason 40
   Thyatira 45
   Is there no King in Thee 50
   The Biblical Paradigm of Gentile Brides ... 55
   Abandoned by God 60
   After the Harpazo 65
   Where Have We Gone 70
Grace 75
   The Virtuous Woman 77
   The Paradigm of Jehu 82

Table of Contents

Iron Mixed with Clay 87
A Man Raised to Know God 92
The Days of Noah 97
Make Thee an Ark 102
Be Fruitful and Multiply 107
From Ham to Nimrod 112
The Patience of Job 117
Job's Reward 122
Jeremiah 10 127
You Who Killed the Prophets 132
Special Operations Wounded Warriors 137
Biography 144

Preface

What if the words of the teacher were absolute and undeniable? What if mathematical probabilities proved coincidence does not exist! What if we are following the carefully devised plan of an intelligent designer of our creation? What if he is ordering the footsteps of everything and every person in his creation? Are we following an ancient pattern?

There is nothing new under the sun. God has written us a warranty deed and owner's manual based upon predestined characters who have manifested in many forms. And at the heart of each Old Testament character, manifests Lucifer's plan to try and halt what God has predetermined.

As the third book in my Becoming series. Becoming Jezebel outlines how a female queen to a man whose family once knew God, convinces his people to abandon the God who delivered them the land, in favor of occult fertility practices that have migrated from Babylon.

Jezebel is the daughter of King Eth Baal. He is the king of the people known as Sidonians. We use their Greek name, the Phoenicians. His capitol is Tyre. His gods are the fallen angels who convinced men to allow their daughters to engage in marital relations and their offspring became the race of giants.

These giants were holders of dual DNA. God had promised his Messiah would be born to a pure Jewish virgin bloodline. Satan was attacking Adam's bloodline to halt God's plan for humanity and his creation.

Eth-Baal is an homage to the Babylonian god Baal. It transliterates as lord in English. He is the chief deity in the Babylonian pantheon and King Eth-Baal is the priest of their fertility religion. His daughter serves at the temple of Asherah.

Baal is the god of fertility, weather, seasons, war, and sailors. Phoenecia boasted enormous wealth from their trade across the Mediterranean and Aegean seas.

They believed Baal was responsible for everything in their lives. Belief in this created deity, advanced paganism to the point where phallic symbols and Babylonian fertility holidays were welcomed in the land God had sanctified for his worship alone.

Jezebel nationalized the fertility cults, and king Ahab welcomed them. Israel had moved so far away from thus says the Lord, that they were willing to sacrifice their children to the god Baal.

In Babylon, human sacrifice of infants was welcomed in the cult of Mithras and Ishtar. Mithras is portrayed as a bull and he is the god of military might and monetary strength. Ishtar is portrayed as half naked woman and half bunny rabbit. The cults of Mithras and Ishtar were thriving in the most holy place on earth.

Jezebel begins her career serving Ahab by pulling off the first inquisition of a Jewish bloodline, for the purpose of seizing a real estate asset. She cuts off every male heir to the land owned by Naboth.

The Palestinian claim to God's land can be traced to the murder of Naboth's family to none other than Jezebel. She brought the house of the moon god back to Jericho during the time of Ahab's rule. Exactly as Joshua was told would happen due to his failure to tear down all of the high places and kill every Nephillim offspring and the sons of men who allowed their daughters to lie with fallen angels.

Now Jezebel has been allowed to propagate her Babylonian cult religion in the house of God on earth. A Jewish king who once knew God, allowed it all to transpire. The pattern has repeated itself in history and the final battle between the house of Jehu and the house of Omri rages here in America.

Ahab and Jezebel have reappeared in America as a president and his fertility cult leader wife. Bill Clinton a man who once boasted of being brought up Southern Baptist, and his wife, a devout eugenicist in the model of Margaret Sangar.

Hillary Rodham Clinton began her career with the murder of Vince Foster to secure her about to be Governor husband a prime piece of Arkansas land. She now has advanced Jezebel's fertility cult at the World Health Organization

Preface

by using U.S. taxpayer money to fund abortion all over the world.

Donald Trump is God's representative from the house of Jehu. It is his sole responsibility to destroy the house of Ahab and Jehoram. Then he can focus on gathering the eagles in Babylon to begin the march toward Revelation 17-18, Isaiah 13-14 and Jeremiah 50-51.

America has gone the way of ancient Israel and we are under the abandonment wrath of God which Paul prophesied would befall the revived Roman empire in this time. Romans 1 begins Paul's rebuke of those who would have the Roman government in any form as their God, proving Trump is Jehu who fails at removing the two golden calves set up by Jeroboam in ancient Israel.

The harbingers of judgement upon ancient Israel have all manifested in the last nineteen years. We are in the Shmita year and I believe we will see a bankruptcy looming on the American horizon. Our dollar will be replaced as the world's reserve currency, and our judgement from God as Sodom and Gomorrah is imminent.

We are Mystery Babylon, the whore which sitteth upon many waters. Our judgement was sealed at Babel when Nimrod led the first rebellion by men following the pattern of his fallen archangel master, Lucifer. He has once again united the world under one language with one reserve currency with portraits of men upon them. We can delude no further.

God has to judge America or he will have to apologize to Sodom and Gomorrah!

Join me as we go behind the veil of eternity to adjudicate how ancient religious practices have entered houses of worship, and our country through the biblical pattern of Jezebel.

America has exactly the same problems ancient Israel faced as they marched further and further away from God's revealed word, toward ancient Babylonian fertility practices. Professing believers were allowing this practice wholesale in Israel and it is part of the American Christian experience as I pen these words.

Let us travel through biblical times and adjudicate if there is nothing new under the sun when it comes to all human religious practices. Only the blood of our Lamb can cleanse America now!

He was crucified upon a cross of wood, yet he created the hill upon which it stood.

He is alive forevermore, and he is coming for his virgin bride soon.

John Burns 5-8-2022.

MERCY

The Time of Jezebel

David was anointed by Samuel to be King of Israel at twelve years of age. He is the son of Jesse and his mother was the Queen of Ammon. Apparently, the Messianic bloodline has been attacked since Cain slew Abel.

David follows in Jessie's footsteps, and has an affair with Bathsheba. She is the wife of David's best general, Uriah the Hittite. Evidence supports that Uriah had converted from Hittite polytheism to Jewish monotheism and the worship of YHWH.

David successfully conspires to kill Uriah through the use of his soon to be rebel general, Joab. Joab has the army of Israel pull back as Uriah leads them at the toughest spot on the battlefield. That must have really hurt Uriah as he was deceived by his own leaders and then his men.

The adulterous love child of David and Bathsheba would die eight days after being born. Is that a coincidence or was God stopping the circumcision right to bring this innocent child home to glory?

David's monarchy would never see peace again. The sword will never depart from the house of David until Jesus Christ is recognized as their risen King. A time of great tribulation is on the near horizon for national Israel. The time of Jacob's trouble, follows the rapture of the bride of Christ. Meta-Tauta!

The offspring of Bathsheba is King Solomon. His mother came to Israel worshipping the gods of her ancestors. She was a moon worshipper from the house of Sheba: today we call it Arabia. The original capitol of the house of the moon god in Judea was Jericho.

Joshua had not finished what God started in Jericho. He allowed for the pagan altars in seven principal cities, to stand. These altars were ancient fertility altars dedicated to serving the fallen angels. Today, the Palestinians still control the seven principal cities, the Judges failed to subjugate, David kills the last giants in Goliaths bloodline under King Saul.

Solomon's sons are split on keeping David's united monarchy intact. Rehoboam is closer to the priest's and religion of his Mosaic ancestors, whilst Jeroboam goes North and allows for pagan occult practices to creep into the land God gave Abraham.

Solomon's kingdom is hopelessly divided between North and South until Messiah unites them under his Star of David and Menorah as his Bride, banner. The kingdom of our God will once again be amongst men! Judah has successive monarchs until taken to Babylon in 586 B.C. The Northern Kingdom will endure several dynastic families.

The bloodline of Messiah is kept intact during the Babylonian captivity. Daniel and his three friends are from the royal line of Judah. Esther saves her people from an inquisition by Israel's oldest enemy, the Amalekites.

Ezra and Nehemiah return to Jerusalem and begin to build the temple and the walls of the city as Greece and Egypt are being challenged by fledgling Rome. Soon after Rome asserts itself in Judea during the time of Messiah, Paganism from Babylon has united under one empire with incredible western expansion awaiting them.

The Religion of Jezebel was welcomed in Samaria and later Jerusalem, and it was welcomed in Rome until Constantine marries the religion of Babylon with the government in Rome. Mithras and Ishtar were united and given the Roman names Jupiter and Aphrodite.

Ahab has ascended to the throne in Israel by murder and paganism. His father reigned on the throne because his father had killed the King. Now Ahab is allowing for the practices of the original usurper to take hold in Israel.

Jeroboam allowed for sodomy amongst the pagans who were not conquered. Apparently, this perversion eventually made its way into Jewish homes also. Ahab has allowed his wife Jezebel to set up phallic symbols in Samaria and groves complete with temple prostitutes litter northern Israel. No wonder the Samaritan woman at the well had five husbands?

Ahab has allowed for the same perversions as Jeroboam when the Davidic monarchy was first divided. Israel had been dedicated to the God of creation, the religion he gave the Hebrews descended from Adam, had led to the construction of their temple in Israel.

Solomon built the temple that David had spent his life pondering over. He gathered the tradesman under Hiram of Tyre. He too worshipped the Phoenician pantheon while building the Jewish temple to YHWH. Solomon gave us the practice of polygamy within circles of people who claim belief in the God of the Bible.

How could God possibly bring an unblemished offspring of the line of Judah with so many Pagan brides? For all intents and purposes, on the surface, it seemed as though Lucifer was succeeding in getting Israel to worship the works of their hands and the strength of their military.

These same two golden calves set up in Samaria by Jeroboam, have followed the Jews of the diaspora to America. The times of Ahab and Jezebel, look a lot like the times we are living in. Ahab and Jezebel have set up shop, and the northern dominated democratic government in America, believes they can beat God!

The war against southern Christian heritage was begun in Babel, and migrated all over the globe, now has its home in modern Pergamos, New York City. Mithras is alive and well protecting wall street and our military might is proclaimed to be second to none. What does scripture say?

Our nation was divided hopelessly after the civil war. Northern Catholics and moon worshipping Muslims, have united with the cult of Mithras masquerading as the republican and democratic party in America. They are united in stopping the gospel from being preached in America and the seeds of paganism are being watered by Ahab and Jezebel.

Is there another inquisition happening in Planned Parenthood clinics all across America? According to our Bible, Ahab and Jezebel are a symptom of all that has gone wrong in America and our judgement is on our near horizon.

He was crucified upon a cross of wood yet he created the hill upon which it stood.

He is alive forevermore, and he is returning for his virgin bride very soon.

John Burns 5-8-2022.

EthBaal King of Tyre

We learn of the father of Jezebel in the book of Kings. Chapter 16 has us introduced to Ahab being chastened by God, for continuing the practices of Jeroboam. Ahab went a step further. He married the daughter of a king who was the head of the largest fertility cult in Canaan.

EthBaal is king of the people identified as Sidonians. Jesus Christ identifies an ancient war between God and these people. Nimrod had consolidated the worship of all things created in Babel. Now, Ishtar and Baal have migrated to the coasts of Israel and modern Lebanon.

Mesopotamia, and more so Babel, is where the fallen angels under the direction of their Archangel leader Lucifer, began to produce offspring with the daughters of Adam. From Babel in Assyria, and Egypt in Mizraim, fallen angels populated all areas in the levant. Canaan was not spared.

The Sidonians were ancient seafaring peoples who established a vibrant trading country we today call Lebanon. Tyre is where EthBaal became King and lord over the ancient fertility religion of Ishtar. Jezebel was his daughter who served at the temple and placed in charge of the offerings of babies from Hebrew mothers.

God warned Israel about the fate that would befall a nation that destroyed their offspring. Israel had allowed for the gods of Babylon and Egypt into their homes and eventually by 586 BC, carved Idols they worshipped were being hidden by Levite priests in the temple dedicated to YHWH.

Baal is the Assyrian and Chaldean word that transliterates into English as lord. He would take on many prefixes and suffixes depending on the created deity he controlled. The oldest cult to incorporate Baal worship is the cult of Mithras. This is the cult of the Bull.

A bull is a beast of burden and animal of sacrifice in antiquity. The bull represented a nations financial stability. The bull always leads to the worship of the towers. The towers are how men expressed how they got wealthy by depending on Mithras the bull. The adherents were called Mithraidites.

The first letter of the Hebrew alphabet is the Aleph. It is the English letter A. It is the first letter in the creation name of God. The Aleph is the Ox. In antiquity, the letter Aleph looked like a two horned beast. God is both our burden bearer and our eventual sacrifice for sins. Calling on Baal, activates God's greatest jealousy as creator.

Jesus Christ once taught he is the Alpha and Omega. This is Greek. What Messiah said in Hebrew was I am the Aleph and the Tau. He was identifying as the Aleph of creation who intended to become our beast of sacrifice. He alone is Lord, not Baal! The Tau is the last letter in the Hebrew alphabet. It represents a cross shaped mark.

The Tau is the mark of Cain. It is where the plan of God was finished. The cross is the only mark in history that sanctified a wedding covenant, and promised a kingdom. Place the cross of Christ squarely at the center of every biblical question, and unbelief in Jesus Christ as God will fade away.

King EthBaal continued what Nimrod started and every empire in history continued. He melded religion with the government. The religion of men was the religion of the state and EthBaal was their leader. The marriage of religion to government was continued.

EthBaal raised Jezebel to be a devout antisemite. She would do anything to get rid of the prophets and priests of YHWH. The problem was, the religious leaders of the day were aiding and abetting her in the destruction of human offspring. Abortion backed by government was codified in Babylon, and continued by the Sidonians of Phoenecia.

Tyre was the center of the Phoenecian world. There were elaborate temples to Ishtar and Baal everywhere. There were schools of learning dedicated to indoctrinating children into the religion of the state of Phoenecia. Only one education was tolerated, and polytheism was the accepted religion of the state.

Very wealthy elite peoples sent their children to state sponsored schools to learn human fertility practices, and military or financial training. Trade guilds sprung up in Tyre, centered around the worship of Baal and Ishtar. Parents sent their children to learn from a socio-political, elite crowd of people, who controlled every aspect of their lives. Their lives centered around the sacrifice of human children on superheated altars.

No one could question the religious practices of the state of Phoenecia without fear of persecution from within government. Government only allowed one way of thinking, and murder of infants satisfied their need for human suffering. Death is the center of their religious beliefs. All else is secondary.

Phoenecia was incredibly wealthy. No one needed the God of creation. Immorality was at the center of every decision EthBaal made. Perversion of God our creator's family unit, centered around human sacrifice, homosexuality, the making of male eunuchs, which was an ancient transgender practice.

The fallen angels were causing God's people to mock him as creator. The priests of God were silent as they became incredibly wealthy. Synagogues were popping up all over, and the acceptance of a watered-down religious experience became mainstream in Israel. Nothing has changed in America.

Religious traditions replaced relationship to God as creator. Ancient fertility holidays were accepted in Hebrew religious services. Christmas and Easter, replaced Passover, and the resurrection according to God's calendar in the Torah. Shabbat was changed to Sunday, and slaves were given Sunday off to worship at the houses of sun gods.

EthBaal required men worship his opinion about what Moloch accepts as a sacrifice. His opinion was centered in human death. God hates EthBaal, and Jezebel is alive and well today. Hillary Clinton will make her return for the purpose of being destroyed by the house of Jehu in 2024!

He was crucified upon a cross of wood, yet he created the hill upon which it stood.

He is alive forevermore, and he is returning for his virgin bride very soon.

John Burns 5-13-2022.

Jereboam I

Jesus Christ taught that a little leaven, leavens the whole lump. Our God promised to redeem his creation through the seed of the woman. In biology, women have no seed. Our salvation has always been based upon a supernatural creator, saving us through his supernatural blood transfusion begun at Calvary in 32 AD. It never runs low!

Elohim had set in motion a predetermined plan to redeem mankind in the original garden. That garden housed a single tree that man was asked not to touch. 3,000 years later, God would allow himself to be crucified upon the same tree, in the same garden.

Biblical patterns are most important when trying to understand faith in Jesus Christ. Every word in scripture has happened, is happening, or will eventually happen. Every letter, every part of speech, and every number was placed in the Bible by a loving designer. You can find yourself in the lives of Old Testament characters.

Jeroboam is a most interesting character. Within two generations of God establishing David's monarchy, rebellion has taken place away from the worship of God as creator.

Jeroboam had denied Rehoboam's succession to Israel's throne and led an expedition north to establish a divided monarchy with ten tribes following Jeroboam.

Has anything changed with denominational Christianity in America? After all, it was Baptists and Lutherans who persecuted Puritans and Jews in Europe leading to our nation's founding by people who loved the Bible. Every word of it. The Puritans alone did not separate Jesus Christ from his distinctly Jewish future.

Jeroboam convinced 87% of Israel to forgo the truth of the word of God, in favor of melding a little bit of God with pagan religious observances. It is he who set up the two golden calves that haunt our nation today, and will eventually lead to the apostacy by church folk very soon.

Calves are the offspring of bulls. The bull is the oldest cult in the world. Men began to sacrifice bulls before going to war. It is the bull who religious men place their hope in. The golden calf was the mocking of God's plan to become the beast of burden to be sacrificed upon the cross. The golden calf mocks God's plan to become the son of God in the womb of Mary.

Jeroboam set up the first golden calf in Bethel. A careful study using the Hebrew hermeneutics Jesus Christ used, reveals the name of God's house is Bethel. The golden calf was brought into the house of God in Bethel. Abram had set up the first altar for the worship of Elohim in Bethel, now Jeroboam was mocking God by setting up a pagan idol in God's house.

Denominational churches have done the same thing in America as they mix Roman religious holidays and observances with a little bit of Jesus the man. Allowing the state into our church services denies that God supplies all of our needs according to his riches in Glory. Money has become the God of Nicaolaitin preachers in churches all across our land.

The Northern kingdom set up by Jeroboam is a prophetic reference to what has happened to belief in Messiah here in America. Professing believers have no power in ministry because the golden calf of monetary solvency is more important than leading people under the blood of the Lamb.

Jeroboam had returned the Jewish people to pagan religious practices and God was very angry. The nation he had birthed to become a shining city on a hill, was now acting exactly like the pagans they were asked to separate from. God alone sanctified Israel, and he is today getting ready to redeem his covenant people in Israel again, as he closes the door to Gentile salvation.

The second golden calf set up by Jeroboam occurred in the town of Dan. The tribe of Dan are the warrior tribe. It was Dan who led all the attacks on Israel's enemies when they entered the promised land. It was Dan who was assigned the eagle as his banner. It was Dan who was given the job of crushing the head of the serpent with the Word of God, yet Dan relied wholly on military might and forgot the God who actually fought the battles for them.

It was Jeroboam who introduced the Jewish people to homosexuality. It was punishable by death in the ancient world, for population was power and to partake in homosexuality was an abomination to our creator. God cannot use a homosexual because they are too selfish to reproduce and provide God with worshippers.

Silent pulpits in ancient Israel contributed to the decline in Biblical morality. Rabbis and prophets had gotten comfortable relying on their own ability to provide for themselves and their mighty military gave them a sense of comfort that led to wholesale denial of God's covenants. Today, church denies every covenant God sealed in the Old Testament, in favor of allowing the golden calves of Jeroboam, comfort, in the houses of worship, God is not in.

Jeroboam capitulated totally away from absolute morality established by God in eternity past. It was he who allowed the worship of the gods of Bathsheba, and Solomons 300 wives, and many concubines into the house of God. Compromise began in Israel with the worship of the golden calf of Egypt in the desert of Midian.

This single act of defiance led to a gradual decline in morality, and Jeroboam's plan was to double down. He led Israel completely away from the worship of the creator in favor of worshipping all things God created. Pride filled Jeroboam, and humility in worship was lost in favor of Jeroboam's own ability to provide for Israel through warfare and money.

Nothing has changed in the America I love. Church is comfortable worshipping at the altar of Israel's two golden calves. America is no different. The harbingers of judgement that manifest in ancient Israel, have all manifested in the America I love, and still the church doubles down in pride.

Jesus Christ must return soon to rescue his bride from within the body of Christ which has followed the ancient pattern of falling away from sound Hebrew doctrines outlined by God in the Old Testament. The church in America will soon be shocked as God removes Christ's promised Bride and they are left behind to worship the cult of human government.

He was crucified upon a cross of wood, yet he created the hill upon which it stood.

He is alive forevermore, and he is returning for his virgin bride very soon.

John Burns 5-14-2022.

North South Conundrum

It is no coincidence America fought a civil war. Our nation is a direct pattern of the nation of Israel. We share the distinction of having our nation dedicated to the God of the Bible. Both Israel and America were dedicated to God and his perfect will for the lives of its citizens.

Israel as a nation was predestined to be God's covenant people who were to birth and eventually crucify the Messiah. America was birthed solely for two purposes: taking the gospel of Jesus Christ to the four corners of the earth, and protecting the remnant of Jewish immigrants here in America until God would regather them for the second time.

Israel was founded in Egyptian bondage. America was founded under pagan monarchial rule, and denominational bondage to human religion. Israel was given the Torah and law to show all of us exactly what we need saving from. America was given the Bible to teach the world God's two divine attributes he offered on Calvary, mercy and grace.

Israel entered the desert after Egyptian servitude totaling 400 years. God told Abram his descendants would be strangers in a pagan land. That is their conundrum currently. Israel was deported to the four corners of the earth, for compromising with the pagan world around them, and allowing foreign gods into their lives and places of worship.

David was God's man to rule Israel after they chose Saul whom God abandoned. David would unite the Hebrews in the land God had promised them, but he did nothing to finish the conquest of Joshua and pagan altars permeated the tribes of the northern Kingdom. A little leaven, began to leaven the whole lump of Israel, set apart by God, for his purposes alone.

David committed adultery with Bathsheba a Hittite. He conspired to have her husband, Uriah murdered and in turn, persuaded his general to also become a murderer. David had Uriah murdered by Joab and at the end of his life, David would have to warn Solomon that Joab needed to be executed. One bad decision in David's life led to a series of covenant breaking actions by the only man in the Bible that God says is a man after, mine own heart. In both testaments!

Now David had a wife who would bring in all kinds of abominable Babylonian practices into Monotheistic belief in Israel. The people God had chosen for his purposes, were all doing what was right in their own eyes. Nothing has changed in America! No country on Earth has believers compromise with 87% of scripture like denominational churches in America.

David's son Solomon took hundreds of wives, and hundreds more concubines for his perversion. Solomon birthed polygamy in monotheism. God's way has always been one man with one woman for life. Churches leads the way in divorce in America, and according to their own statistics, the Southern Baptist Convention boasts of a whopping 59% divorce rate amongst attendees in their first marriage.

I wonder if it has something to do with denying Jesus Christ's coming kingdom? I wonder if racism and antisemitism has played a role in the denial of 87% of scripture in America, in favor of pagan religious observances? Will water baptism count for anything, if the Baptist churches do not move away from antisemitic Bible interpretation?

Churches have become so heavenly minded in America they are no earthly good. The worship of ancestors is more important than the belief in all of the Bible. They judge others guilty while giving themselves a pass because they do what government tells them, to begin with worshipping on the first day of the work week in God's Bible.

Sunday is a pagan day of work. Shabbat established by God is always Friday evening through Saturday evening. All having to do with the cycles of the moon, not the worship of the sun!

Israel became hopelessly divided between north and south within 70 years of being in the land and prospering. America suffered the same fate and for the same reasons. Northern pagans now control the flow of information to southern Christian homes. It begins with public education in preschool.

After the south was forced to surrender, northern bankers looked to consolidate power through political parties in

America. Neither is on the side of the God of the Bible. If they were, the Bible would never be legislated out of our children's lives. Prayer would still be allowed each time a school starts its day.

Public educators have taken part in the fleecing of America and they have advanced an immoral agenda with our tax dollars. Jesus Christ would never go to public school!

Our schools have become indoctrination factories where the existence of God as creator is denied by every evolutionary thinking teacher at odds with the God of the Bible. Charles Darwin has replaced Jesus Christ in the lives of your children, and yes public-school teachers have taken part, knowingly!

Northern politicians now control the democratic party of the ancestors of southerners who once fought to keep Jesus Christ in the lives of our citizens. Their agenda includes the dumbing down of our children and the total movement away from God's morality as outlined in the Bible.

Silent pulpits have contributed to societies move away from the family unit established by God in Genesis. Alternate sexuality, and immorality is being advanced by eugenic minded teachers who take part in teaching your children to choose their gender as early as third grade. These teachers may look good on the outside, but on the inside, they desire to get you and Jesus Christ out of your child's life.

Can adults who support infant euthanasia be trusted with the education of our most vulnerable citizens? Does the northern democratic way, support the rich Christian heritage enjoyed by most southerners who love Jesus Christ?

Israel and Judah have been hopelessly divided for over 2,500 years because they allowed pagans to hijack their children's lives. Israel was abandoned by God for a season, and I fear America has been abandoned by God as well. Repent and return your children to both testaments of scripture and revival can begin in America!

He was crucified upon a cross of wood, yet he created the hill upon which it stood.

He is alive forevermore and he is returning for his virgin bride very soon.

John Burns 5-14-2022.

From Jezebel to Planned Parenthood

What has contributed to the moral collapse we are witnessing in our nation? How are we as born-again believers supposed to view our dilemma?

God alone established civilization upon entropy laws at creation. Five days God set about reducing chaos and establishing perfect order in our world, and all for the purpose of placing man in a garden to teach the world his single plan of redemption.

Our Bible is the most amazing science textbook ever assembled. Sixty-six books, revealed to 40+ men over 2,500 years, all pointing to the cross of Christ. God wrote a love story in eternity past, then revealed his plan to the nation of Israel beginning with Moses in the wilderness of Midian.

The Old Testament is the foundation upon which God framed our entire story. The characters of the Old Testament all point to the incredible need for God's eternal mercy. As Long as we exist in the presence of sin, mercy should be what we ask for daily. God offers no one grace until they have the humility to repent daily, and request mercy.

Jezebel is a villain in the Old Testament whom Jesus Christ assigns the task of aiding him in teaching all of us what went wrong with church. Thyatira is recognized by Messiah as the middle age church of Rome who plotted an inquisition against the Jewish people. Jezebel is a pattern that now is being fulfilled in the life of Hillary Rodham Clinton.

Jesus Christ identifies Thyatira as being an unbroken chain of females who have led men away from monotheism toward polytheism, and the worship of the woman and her womb. Jezebel planted seeds that have manifested in these days, and people in church support the abortion of babies so they are not inconvenienced to raise children.

Ahab was king of the northern tribes of Israel. Jeroboam allowed for pagan fertility altars to reopen for business. Ahab has a unique name from God. His name transliterates as Father's Brother. This is an allusion to the ancestor worship that had taken hold in Israel, that Jesus Christ tried to correct. By the advent of Messiah, Israel thought it was more important to worship Abraham, a lot more than worship God.

Nimrod began to allow men to worship him as a God, and Israel followed suit. Today, men worship all kinds of human deities they have venerated to include preachers. Everyone has itching ears, and forgo the truth of the anointing of God upon our lives. God's Holy Spirit alone should be our guide and the Bible should be solely what we place our hope in, not men's opinions about the Word. Including mine!

Semiramis was the consort and wife of Nimrod. She is the seed Lucifer planted in Babel that has led to the deification of the woman. She demanded equality in women, and her tool was to convince women to rebel against God's will for women as the primary role of teaching children God's plan of redemption. God alone exalts women to be the purveyors of grace within the marriage covenant.

Nothing is more important to God than raising children to worship and glorify him as creator. Men and women have unique qualities from our creator. The purpose of God for allowing the marriage of one man to one woman for life, is to provide him with Godly seed. Sports have replaced the need for God in the lives of our children, and athletes are now more important than God our creator.

What does it mean to be Godly? I have watched Christians wear bracelets with the letters WWJD on them. I like to think about what Jesus Christ did not do. Jesus Christ never shamed anyone into belief in him. He came into the world to save sinners. He offered only mercy and grace. Why do preachers believe it is their job to teach church folk to judge others sin and not their own?

Because shaming people sells seats. There is a lot of market share gained when we segregate to kidnap God for a few hours each week. Judging others is always easier than asking God to correct our thinking about all things Jesus. Jezebel brought Babylon into church, and Christians are more comfortable following a pagan holiday schedule, than allowing the word of God to correct them.

What is so sinister about the unbroken chain of women being comfortable murdering the child God has given them? How can Christians support alternate morality? Why has emotion replaced the hard truths of the Bible? The clue lies in God's eternal mercy.

The Hebrew word found in our Old Testament denoting eternal mercy is Rachamim. The I'm on the end denotes a dual meaning, and provides the tools to understand why God hates abortion, and those who support its barbarism.

The first meaning is obvious to most believers, mercy. To not receive what we all deserve, for the wages of sin is death. Mercy is what is missing in Christian testimony as preachers have taught their congregations to pervert grace, just like Jesus Christ said would happen.

The key of mercy alone opens the door of grace. Grace is unmerited favor from God, distributed freely to all those who have the courage to ask for mercy daily. God's mercy is unending, church mercy is non-existent!

Church people judge pregnancy out of wedlock. Jesus Christ says I will have mercy and not sacrifice. Pray for mercy over the lives of pregnant single women, and grace will again appear in our society.

The second meaning of Rachamim is incredible! The root word is Recham. It is the sole place mercy begins in all of our lives. Recham is the WOMB of the woman. She alone has been exalted by God for the purpose of raising children to show unending mercy. The womb of women is where God intended to carry out his whole plan as he exalted Mary the virgin to be the mother of Messiah.

To empower women is to become Godly men again, and remember that God gave us an incredible gift in women, and she is the only part of creation that God says was really good!

He knows the plans for your child before conception begins. God is sovereign over the womb of women, and men who are courageous will support women in all their endeavors that provide children with the foundation of mercy.

The grace of women alone, teach our children Jesus Christ's desire to show our creation his unending mercy. Teshuva Christian men! Repent and return to the entire Bible message and let's get back to offering what Jesus Christ first offered his creation, unending mercy from the creator who became a man in the womb of a virgin Jewish girl.

He was crucified upon a cross of wood, yet he created the hill upon which it stood.

He is alive forevermore, and he is returning for his virgin bride very soon.

John Burns 5-16-2022.

For this Reason

Genesis 2:24 begins with God proclaiming, there is only one reason he allows for the marriage covenant between one man and one woman for life. What is the single reason our God gave us human sexuality inside the covenant of marriage? Are God's thoughts ever man's thoughts?

For this reason, shall a man leave his father and mother, and cleave to the bosom of his wife, and the two shall become one flesh. Human intercourse within marriage is God's gift to us. Render unto each other due benevolence, so that the tempter, tempt ye not. Romans 6.

One flesh begins between a man and woman, only when a man has the courage to leave the trappings of home, and learn without momma, to care for the woman God has rewarded you with. She is to become the glory of man, only when men listen to her, more than listen to momma.

Why was Abraham commanded by God to leave his home in Mesopotamia? Why was it so important to God to separate Abram for his purposes? What was Abram's reaction?

At the time of Abram, the Chaldean, Babylon was the predominate religion, and Assyria and Egypt vied for power over the thriving fertile crescent of commerce. The ancient Babylonian pantheon begun by Nimrod and Semiramis was thriving in Abram's world. Might his parents have been polytheists?

Abram defied God, and only moved a little up river to Haran, and awaited the death of his father, so he could bury him in the land of his nativity. Abram defied God in worshipping his ancestors, more than trust the sovereign word of God. Abram's problems travel with him to Canaan.

When Abram arrives, there is a famine in the land. The same land God had promised Abram would be a land flowing with milk and honey. Doubt now crept into Abram's thoughts and he moves his family into the other pagan capitol of the ancient world, Egypt. Now he deceives Pharoah.

Abram plays a ruse. His wife Sarai is so beautiful, he convinces her to pretend she is his sister, to gain favor with the priest and king of Egypt, Pharoah. This man who believed he was a god, figured out that Sarai was Abram's wife, when he and his family began to experience plagues. Was adultery not an acceptable practice in ancient Egypt?

Pharoah confronts Abram. Why did ye not tell me she was thy wife, had I not had her for myself? He was worried about the punishment for committing adultery in Egypt. To the ancient Egyptians, population was power in military might, and power in leveraging and levying taxes. Men and Women were asked to have many children.

Adultery was punishable by death in Egypt and ancient Assyria, who both required incredible populations to afford their military and their civil affairs people with soldiers, artisans, craftsmen, farmers, fisherman and slaves.

Faithfulness to one wife ensured, children only ever learned Egypt and Assyria's gods respectively. The mother was responsible for teaching children who their father believed in. Dad's gods, were the family's gods.

Mom was respected and loved by dad because they alone were raising their children to be productive citizens. Both mom and dad were required in the ancient world that was the beginning of civilization. Each was equal in pro-genitor-ship, or what we call child rearing.

These two ancient civilizations teach us a lot about what has gone wrong in America with the family God alone ordained to be the cornerstone of creation. Why was Abram so willing to lie about being married? Why did Sarai go along with the ruse?

Had Mesopotamia migrated with Abram with the perversion of God's marriage covenant through alternative morality learned in Babylon? Abram was called by God, communed with God, yet he mocked God twice before cutting the Abrahamic covenant. Something had to change for God to use pre-destined Abram the gentile.

For Abram to become Abraham, the anointing of God had to overcome his religious pre-suppositions, learned from his ancestors, and that required the baptism of the Holy Spirit. Abram needed the Ruah ha Khodesh of God.

He needed the injection of the H in he and Sarai's life, indicating God intended to anoint them both with the third person of the Trinity. The same requirement today, if you intend to fulfill God's perfect pleasing will in your life. This is the perfect illustration of how God views Israel through the lens of Abraham, and how he sees the bride of Christ through the eyes of Sarai.

Abraham was promised that his descendants would occupy the land of Israel forever. He is called the father of many nations. Be careful to differentiate between the descendants of Abram the gentile and Abraham the Hebrew.

In the story of Abraham, we are introduced to the unnamed servant in his house. We later learn that servants name: Eleazar. His name transliterates as comforter. It is he, whom Abraham sends into the pagan land of his ancestors to find his chosen son a virgin bride.

It is our story, as God has sent the comforter into our world to find his son a virgin bride, and his church worships the pantheon of Roman gods while claiming to serve only Jesus Christ.

God has always allowed one man to be with one woman because he was seeking Godly seed. Godly seed are children instructed in the truths of the Bible beginning in Genesis, ending in Revelation. Godly seed understand our Messiah from the Old Testament view of mercy.

Every perversion of the marriage covenant instituted by God in Genesis, can be traced to monotheism compromising with the polytheist world around them. Has anything changed? Have American denominational preachers allowed pagan religious practices into their professed houses of Christian worship?

Actually, America has a lot said about it in scripture, once you leave denominational religious traditions behind in the Roman church world. Repent and return to both edges of Jesus Christ's professed sword, which is the word of God, given to all of us for the vanquishing of the enemies of God in the lives of all those we encounter.

He was crucified upon a cross of wood, yet he created the hill upon which it stood.

He is alive forevermore, and he is returning for his virgin bride very soon.

John Burns 5-20-2022.

Thyatira

This is a feminine pronoun. It is the Greek rendering of the Babylonian name of Semiramis. She was the consort of Nimrod, the world's first dictator who set up his kingdom on the banks of the Euphrates River in ancient Sumer. His capitol was Babel. This proper locative name transliterates into English as: We will rebel.

What did Nimrod specifically rebel from? He is labeled as a mighty hunter. He is a descendant of Ham through Cush. We know that Ham performed a homosexual act upon Noah, leading to the sons of Ham being cursed to a life of servitude to their two older brothers.

Nimrod committed adultery. He took the wife of one of his generals as his own. Her name is Semiramis. She is the mother of every fertility cult on earth. She led women away from God's one plan for their life, to be the mothers of all the living. Her tools were the night sky, the sun and the moon.

Enoch had taught Methuselah and the preflood patriarchs God's single plan of redemption, by viewing the twelve constellations in their order of brightness. He was the world's first biblical astronomer. The twelve-star constellations were incorporated into our Bible, so all men could be without excuse.

Job gives them the title of the Mazzaroth in chapter 38 of his book. Beginning with a virgin and ending with a lion ruling over the entire earth. Greek astrology and Pagan mythology can be rightly understood from human history alone. The story of the Gospel comes alive in the stars when we understand history and we love and fear God as creator.

Semiramis eventually has Nimrod killed to place her son, through an adulterous affair with a fallen angel, on the throne of Nimrod who has named himself as the god over creation. Moloch is deified as half man and half Bull. The mocking of God as creator began with Nimrod and Semiramis.

All pagan religious calendars and all pagan religious practices mock God as sole creator. Nimrod gave us the birth of his son Tammuz on the 25th day of the 12th month on the Babylonian lunisolar calendar. It was celebrated when the planet Saturn could be visually spotted in the morning sky.

Lucifer is given the homage from God as the son of the morning. Fallen angels are often referenced by the star constellations they worshipped as their place of origin. Lucifer's star can be seen in every home where Christians celebrate the Babylonian legend of Christmas.

It was during this festival, that Babylonians who worshipped Lucifer would cut down an Erez tree, decorate it with silver and gold, place a star as an homage to the son of the morning upon it, then have an elaborate meal sacrificed to the idols of Tammuz, Ishtar, Nimrod, Moloch, Sin, Nebo, and every other pagan deity from Babylon.

Nimrod celebrated the birth of his son on the day we tell people God's son was born? I wonder often if God will forgive people who mock his plan, especially when they turn their children into covetous beggars? Jeremiah 10 identifies Christmas as a heathen practice and a reason God has decided to judge Israel for allowing them to migrate into monotheistic worship of YHWH.

A little leaven had leavened the entire lump just like it has in supposed houses of Christian worship in America. It began at our second founding, when extremely eugenic, slaveholding men compromised with the God of the Bible and began a country of, for, and by a people who always intended to get God's morality out of their lives.

Who needs God when we have all this freedom that $1/10^{th}$ of 1 percent of the population has paid for in war? Our true veterans are those who have served a cause greater than themselves, and returned home to find most Americans prostituting the freedom purchased by the blood of true American sons and unfortunately daughters in war.

In Babylon on the winter solstice, Nimrod and Semiramis began to celebrate their son's birthday. His name is Tammuz I. He was given the title son of the gods. The spotting of Saturn in the morning of the winter solstice, when the sun was reborn and daylight increased a little more each day. This was seen as an omen to the Babylonian high priest who assumed the title Pontifex Maximus.

Christmas was born in Babylon. To celebrate the birth of Tammuz, women brought their infant children to be sacrificed on superheated bronze altars, as an homage to Abed Nego. He is the priest given the title of servant of Lucifer.

Luciferianism has its roots in Christmas from Babylon. The logs they burned were called yule logs. The word yule is Chaldean. It transliterates as infants. So, yes, Nimrod and Semiramis gave us infanticide leading to abortion on demand and paid for by believers, disguised as planned parenthood.

Semiramis began a fertility cult that erected phallic symbols around these altars on all of the high places in Babylon. They built elaborate groves that venerated the woman's womb, and reproductive cycles. The name of their goddess was Ishtar.

Her statue was the body of a virgin woman with the head of a bunny rabbit. She guarded a golden egg, symbolizing the perversion of the seed of the woman prophesied by God to crush the head of the serpent. Her medium for followers was to supply chocolate which in ancient Babylon, was believed to be a fertility drug. Contraception had its roots in Babylon.

Thyatira is the name Jesus Christ identified as his fourth church. It is the place where Luciferianism gained a foothold in the body of Christ. Pergamos is where the Church entered an unholy marriage to the world around them. In Thyatira they were engaging in all kinds of pagan rituals and holidays that God hates. Jezebel and Ahab are their ancestral reasons.

These two people are responsible for every inquisition upon Jewish people ever purported. When they are left behind at the rapture, they once again will persecute the Jewish remnant left in America and the rest of the fallen world.

Make sure your beliefs in Jesus Christ have nothing to do with the practices of those caught in bondage to Babylonian religious cult practices. You will know them first by how much they blame everyone else, and never look in their own church mirror.

He was crucified upon a cross of wood, yet he created the hill upon which it stood.

He is alive forevermore, and he is returning for his virgin bride very soon.

John Burns 5-20-2022.

Is there no King in Thee

Prerequisite to receiving a kingdom, the proposed prince is often given a bride chosen by his father. Our Messiah, the Prince of Peace, will one day receive a kingdom, but first, God must find him a willing gentile bride from all the nations of the earth.

In our story, a king in Israel has chosen the wrong bride. She continues the pattern of men chosen by God for his purpose, mocking him, by allowing the wife to emigrate paganism with all of the fertility cults into the lives of people chosen by God to worship only him.

The pollution of Jezebel and the Sidonian pantheon into Israel, has never allowed that great nation to fulfill God's perfect pleasing will for their lives. Not even separation from their land for 1830 years without a Temple to worship YHWH in, has chastened the Hebrews into belief in Yeshua.

Israel's history is marred with kings' men chose, not chosen by God. They seem to always get it wrong the first time, then have to be chastened to the point of near extinction, before asking for eternal mercy. There is a fulfillment of prophecy yet future for the nation of Israel. Isaiah 11:11 proves this.

In Acts 6 Stephen takes the pharisees through a Bible history class. He uses the patriarchs and Moses as his classroom. He reminds them that in each case our forefathers got it wrong the first time and only after chastening by God, did they repent and get it right the second time. This is a Biblical paradigm.

None greater than Saul and David.

Abraham had been predestined to be the patriarch of the nation known in the Bible as Israel. He alone was taken by God up Mount Moriah to teach him the only way a man can ever be counted righteous. The Akedah is the most misunderstood teaching in Christian circles. Yet it alone teaches true faith in God!

Abraham was taken behind the veil of eternity to learn the heart and single plan of God. He is told to take his one and only son, the heir to all Abraham is entitled to from God, and sacrifice him ritually as Adam had been shown in the garden. Isaac freely bears the wood to be burned under his body after his father prepared to pierce his side with a knife.

Abraham travels three days to the place in Jerusalem where he will willingly offer his son. He instructs his two young helpers to stay here while he and the lad go to worship God and return unto them.

Was Abraham lying after being tempted by God? Or did Abraham's faith leave him unwavering in understanding God will have to raise Isaac from the dead to keep the covenant he gave him?

When Abraham and Isaac reach the place of the sacrifice, Isaac poses a question of the father he loves. Father, we have the wood for the sacrifice but where is the lamb?

Abraham and Isaac were playing out what Messiah would utter from the garden before his sacrifice; Father, if it is possible, let this cup passeth, not my will, but thy will be done. Another willing son with total faith in what the father would accomplish through his death, burial, and resurrection.

As Abraham binds his willing son, then raises the knife, God himself intervenes. He alone will provide himself as the lamb! God revealed his intention to be the lamb slain for the sins of the world in 32 AD in Jerusalem on the same hill where Abraham and Isaac went to sacrifice unto God.

As Abraham and Isaac return from the sacrifice, Eleazar is instructed to load ten camels and ride into the land of his nativity to find his son a willing, gentile, virgin bride. The camels were for the dowry to be paid to the potential bride to be. Our dowry was paid on Calvary. Eleazar transliterates as Comforter!

Isaac and Rebekah would give birth to Easu and Jacob. One accepted and one eternally hated by God. Jacob would go on to be the father of the twelve tribes. Reuben would lose his inheritance through an adulterous act.

Levi becomes the father to the Mosaic priesthood and Judah is given the mantle of birthing the King. Jesus Christ united the two families at his water baptism when he ended the requirement for priests to undertake a mikveh ceremonial immersion bath. The Lamb slain would be raised as the Lion of the tribe of Judah. Water was changed to the wine of forgiveness, when Jesus Christ willingly died on the cross.

Messiah was promised a reward and an inheritance for his willingness to die for the sins of all humanity. His reward is a willing virgin bride, who has not polluted herself with the gods of this world. She is eagerly awaiting the sound of the trumpet, as Messiah will soon be told to go retrieve his bride at the rapture.

Preceding this event is the gentile church age. It has gone on for 1,830 years and counting. During this time, American Christian churches have allowed for the same fertility cults that Jezebel introduced in Israel, to become their Roman church model of traditions where there are no brides being prepared to rule and reign with Jesus Christ in the coming millennium.

Jesus Christ's inheritance is to rule and reign over all of the nations of the earth from Jerusalem for 1,000 literal years. This period of time will be preceded by the tribulation of seven years. The last three and half years is called the time of Jacob's trouble, when the offspring of Jacob will be chastened like never before in human history.

Our story reveals God desiring brides for his kings. Men seem to always choose the wrong queen, that is why God sends the Holy Spirit. If you are the true virgin bride of Christ, then Jesus Christ alone is to be worshipped, and he is only returning to receive a bride who has not committed adultery with the world around them.

He was crucified upon a cross of wood, yet he created the hill upon which it stood.

He is alive forevermore, and he is returning for his virgin bride very soon.

John Burns 5-24-2022.

The Biblical Paradigm of Gentile Brides

Beginning with Eve, God's one plan of redemption revolves around a virgin girl of the house of David, carrying God's seed, to be born King of the Jews. Eve questions God's word, and tries to cover her transgressions with the fig leaves. Church was born in Eden.

God's answer to church was to cover them in the blood of a slain male lamb two years old or younger, and unblemished. His plan for redemption was activated, and Adam was shown the first mercy and grace in human history. He taught Adam his complete plan of redemption by teaching him the semimic contained in the twelve constellations in the night sky.

The Mazzaroth reveals that God always intended to become a lamb in the womb of a virgin girl, to grow up and become the lion of the tribe of Judah, and rule over all the nations of the earth for 1,000 years. God first wrote his plan in the heavens before commissioning Adam and Eve to carry out the plan.

The plan of God to die for the iniquity of humanity, contains eternal mercy in the lives of our Jewish cousins. So many times, had they violated the command to marry only within the tribe. This was exactly why God had to do it all himself. Gentile brides litter the ancestry of Jesus the God-Man.

Noah was perfect in his generation. Cain was no doubt walking the earth prior to the flood bearing the mark of the cross. The TAU is the Hebrew character which denotes a cross. It is the mark of Cain. He could not be killed by anyone but God, and he was marked to be the world that then was, evangelist and teacher.

Noah's sons took wives of the Canaanite women. They had not polluted themselves with fallen angels, and this qualified them to begin repopulation of earth after the flood. This is what made Noah perfect in his generation. He believed God, and it was accounted unto him as righteousness. His water baptism was the flood!

Ham, Shem, and Japheth were instructed to leave the ark and choose a direction of travel. Ham went South by west into Egypt and Africa and in Canaan. Shem settled the fertile plains of Iran, Iraq, Syria, and the Levant, which we call Jordan and Israel, and Lebanon. Japheth went North into the Caucusus mountains of the southern Russian steppes and East into Mongolia and China and lands east of them.

Shem gave birth to Eber in Mesopotamia along the Euphrates River. Eber would be the pro-genitor of Abram and his Gentile wife Sarai. By learning obedience, a Hebrew man and Gentile wife are anointed to become the progenitors of the eventual Messiah from the tribe of Judah. First, they had to escape the world of Nimrod and Semiramis, to begin

God's plan of bringing us the tribe of Jacob for the eventual birth of Jesus Christ.

After the flood of Noah, men began to worship all things God had created. Men deified themselves as the creator god who gave us the earth, the sun, the moon and the 12 stars.

Wives of kings were being worshipped in the cult of Ishtar. This cult belief was given to us by Semiramis when she had intercourse with a fallen angel whom she created a mythology about herself being impregnated by Nebo, the head of the fallen angel cult begun by Lucifer. The religion of Babylon was given to us by a gentile queen calling herself a goddess.

Semiramis gave birth to Tammuz 1 the heir to the throne of Babel on the Euphrates and proclaimed to be the son of god. The pollution of the Mazzaroth taught in Job 38 began in Babel under Nimrod.

Sarai was a descendant of Mesopotamian peoples who allowed the worship of the heavens and fertility in women, by celestial observation. Ziggurats appeared for the viewing of the heavens and the religion of Babel married secular power and our first world dictator who worshipped Mithras the bull was born. The first world order outside of God's plan of redemption for humanity.

Jacob marries gentile Leah and Rachel, while also keeping two gentile concubines. Rachel eventually gives birth to Joseph who is sold into slavery by his brothers for being his mother's favorite shepherd. Joseph takes an Egyptian bride while serving as prime minister. They become the progenitors of the tribes of Ephraim and Manasseh.

Rahab is a citizen of Jericho. When the spies of Israel show up, she makes a shrewd decision to hide them to gain favor with her family. She becomes the eventual great grandmother to kinsman redeemer from Bethlehem, Boaz, who redeems his gentile bride from Moab.

The scarlet thread paradigm was begun in the womb of Rebekah, when Esau had a scarlet thread placed over his toe, when twins were found. God intended to offer salvation to not only the tribe of Jacob, but also every gentile nation on earth.

Jeroboam 1 led the northern kingdom in open rebellion against the plans of God to exalt the offspring of King David when one day Jesus Christ would be born to a virgin Jewish girl. The birth of Jesus Christ is God's answer to men trying to aide Lucifer in stopping the Kingdom of God being established on earth.

God's plan has always involved offering his salvation to all humanity through a Jewish vine and Gentile ingrafting. The pattern continues when Jesus Christ first entrusts gentile Mary Magdalene with the words: I am alive.

We are the virgin gentile bride of Christ only when we forgo the gods men choose and we choose the God of the Bible. His plan of redemption to save gentiles is fast closing. His bride has been invited from all the nations of the earth, to accept his hand in marriage, to fulfill the promise Mary his mother was given while Jesus Christ was in her womb.

We finish the pattern of God accepting gentile brides into his coming kingdom.

He was crucified upon a cross of wood, yet he created the hill upon which it stood.

He is alive forevermore, and he is returning for his gentile bride very soon.

John Burns 5-8-2022.

Abandoned by God

There is a certain wrath spoken of by Paul, that affects the nation called for God's purposes when they chose to relinquish the sovereignty of God over our lives. There are specific symptoms Paul instructs are the final phase of the nation abandoned by God.

The title he chooses is a reprobate mind. The mind that cannot distinguish between moral absolutes and self-relativity. Everyone doing what is right in their own minds. This diagnosis is preceded by the delusion Messiah warned would be poured out in the last days.

Lucifer chose human sexuality and God's first covenant with man, to attack God's single plan of redemption he laid out in the stars of heaven before he brought man into existence. We are all without excuse. Adam and Eve were willing co-conspirators.

When the serpent appears in the garden, he thinks he caught our creator off guard. His rebellion in heaven, continued in Eden when he convinced Adam and Eve to choose religious tradition over faith in God's entire word. Fig leaves are akin to church once or twice a week. The blood of the Lamb is still required if you intend to see God and live!

The marriage covenant established by God in Genesis 2:24, inherently included human intercourse and only with one mate for life. It was Lucifer who attacked the human genome and convinced the daughters of men to mate outside of the marriage covenant.

By Genesis 6, the sons of God were going into the daughters of men creating six fallen angel-human offspring families, with dual DNA. They are called the Nephillim. Their offspring were male, they were warfighters of men, and they were all giants.

Sons of God is only used in the Old Testament to distinguish fallen angels who joined Lucifer in his rebellion. We can become the sons of God, only when we accept Jesus Christ. I believe we are the replacement worshippers God has desired since Lucifer convinced one third of the heavenly host of angels to worship himself.

Jesus Christ said I saw Lucifer fall from Heaven. Peter teaches us One third of the angels were also expelled from heaven. Lucifer now employs them, and Jesus Christ prophesied they are to return soon. Will you recognize the fallen angels courting your daughters?

Such as in the days of Noah, so shall the coming of the son of man be. Genesis 6 explains exactly what was going on at the time of Noah. God had only one covenant and one promise in place by Genesis 6. He had shown Adam how to prepare and sacrifice a lamb for the temporary covering of sin. Messiah would be the last Lamb God will ever allow to be slain!

I have often wondered, is the delusion Jesus Christ identified attached to human sexuality, since it inherently requires us to worship the male and female species? Is the foundation for sin, the perversion of the marriage covenant in any form? I personally believe so.

To condemn the sinner is never the answer. While not accepting sexual perversion in our lives, we are instructed to pray for those caught in bondage to the flesh and nothing more. Jesus Christ offered eternal mercy, and unwavering grace, and so should we! That is what Jesus Christ continues to do.

Ishtar is the feminine deity Jezebel had learned to serve. She is depicted as half bunny rabbit and half virgin girl. She is depicted as possessing a golden egg, denoting her being the deity that gave birth to Tammuz I. He is the son of a fallen angel and the consort of Nimrod.

Her name is Semiramis. It was she who perverted God's plan to birth his son in the womb of a virgin Jewish girl.

Semiramis and Nimrod gave us the cult of fallen angel worship in Babylon. Their son was born on the winter solstice. The holiday venerating his fallen angel father is called Saturnalia. It is when Semiramis convinced the world her husband Nimrod was the creator god who controlled the fallen angel cult run by Lucifer.

The celebration of Nimrod's deification, and the birth of his son, both occurred during the feast of Saturnalia. Usually on the 25th of the 12th month on the Babylonian calendar. This calendar is in direct conflict with the calendar God created all pointing to the first and second coming of Jesus Christ.

Messiah was born on the first of Nisan in spring. On the night the new moon was spotted in Jerusalem. He was circumcised on the 8th of Nisan and presented for inspection by the magi on the 10th of Nisan. He would be crucified on the fourteenth of Nisan. Resurrected on the 17th of Nisan.

The feast of Pentecost was 50 days from the first day of the feast of unleavened bread, when the omer was waved by the priest and counted. Israel would have all their needs met by God's Messiah if they chose to believe.

This leads to the feast of trumpets. One day the Lord will descend with a shout in the clouds. The dead in Christ shall rise, and we which are alive and remain shall be caught up to meet him in the clouds. Messiah will be instructed to go retrieve his bride from within his body.

Trumpets leads to the second coming of Messiah to the earth at the end of the tribulation. At least seven years follows the rapture of the church and Messiah's return to earth to judge all nations who have united to stop his plan of redemption.

This time is known as the time of Jacob's trouble. The only chance for salvation during the tribulation, is martyrdom at the hands of the satanic trinity identified by Daniel in Chapter 2 of his book. Many are called, but few are chosen.

The restrainer has been removed and the most chaotic era in human history begins for all those not counted worthy to become the bride of Christ. He that now letteth shall let, until he be taken out of the way. Without the Holy Spirit during the tribulation, one has only death awaiting their testimony of faith.

He was crucified upon a cross of wood, yet he created the hill upon which it stood.

He is alive forevermore, and he is returning for his virgin bride very soon.

RLTW John Burns 5-28-2022.

After the Harpazo

The most misunderstood Biblical doctrine, is also the one most preachers avoid to their congregation's loss. To understand why the rapture had to occur, is to understand our God, who delights in making and keeping his promises.

The Bible is filled with patterns that lead us to understanding our faith walk. Denominational churches are comfortable holding the world accountable to New Testament theosophy and judgement, while they themselves deny 87% of scripture. At the heart is antisemitism and Greek eugenics.

Jesus Christ was promised by God that he would receive an inheritance and a reward for his death, burial, and resurrection.

Jesus Christ promised reward is a virgin bride taken from all of the nations of the earth. The reason he returned to his father's house to build us a mansion, is because he had to fulfill the Levirite marriage covenant required before a king can receive his kingdom.

Messiah's bride, is identified as a virgin bride which in the Bible is a woman who has not worshipped the pagan gods of this earth in any form. Christmas venerates Lucifer, Easter venerates Ishtar, the bunny rabbit fertility deity. Valentine's Day pollutes the love of God, by confusing it as having to do with Eros, the Roman god of eroticism.

Ecclesiastes proves Jesus Christ never celebrated his birthday. He is the only baby nurtured in the womb of a virgin Jewish girl, born for the single purpose of dying. He wrote the day in advance he was to be crucified. He told our story about the removal of the bride, before the wrath of God is revealed, when he called Noah and his family into the ark. He calls us home, through the cross!

With the collapse of the American dollar now imminent, will Israel be forced to take on the world all by themselves? Pragmatism in politics will require Israel to go on the offensive. Iran has been allowed to develop nuclear weapons by a very naïve and determined socialist demigod at the helm in America.

Our next election will be held while America is filing for bankruptcy and defaulting on its own debt. The dollar will be devalued and hyperinflation will lead to severe famine here in America. Government as God will be found wanting.

Denominational churches will find themselves defending their tax shelters. Business as usual for amillennial churches who denied Jesus Christ's Jewish future in favor of Roman calendar worship. Antisemitism will grip denominations as they once again turn to blaming the Jews to aid the Government in separating them from their property and eventually their lives.

The Psalm 83 war will see Israel finally finish the conquest of Joshua. What Joshua failed to do, led to the times of the Judges, ending with Samuel. Samuel would kill Agag, because Saul did not. His descendants, would persecute Israel many times in history. The failure of the king that men chose, had to be fixed by the king God chose.

The book of Judges ends with Israel's enemies controlling parts of the land God wanted cleansed of all pagan influence. The seven cities that plagued the Judges, still plagues Israel today, and once again the house of the moon god has its capital in Jericho.

The Palestinians control the same cities the descendants of Agag and the other Nephillim offspring controlled. Look to the Palestinians to again worship these men of renown very soon. Jesus Christ prophesied, such as in the days of Noah, so shall the coming of the son of man be.

As Israel looks to Levitically purify the land, they will also begin the building of the millennial temple in the city of David. It sits a few hundred meters south of the dome of the rock. Soon the priests in Israel who are descendants of Aaron and Zadok, shall repent and look once again to God's blueprint.

The world around Israel will look to unite the house of the sun god in Rome, with the house of the moon god in Babylon under a Shiite Mahdi who has waged a war against the Sunni's. I believe the eagles of war shall begin to gather in the valley of Jezreel, stretching from Israel to the west bank of the Euphrates River.

A western leader, out of the western leg of the revived Roman empire, will unite antisemites under the banner of antichrist, which I believe is the Shahada of Islam worn by Hezbollah and the IRGC in Iran. The Shiites have believed their Mahdi has been alive in occultation since 1979 and our introduction to the Ayatollah in Iran.

The religion of Babylon will unite under a secular world leader under the control of Lucifer himself who will form a satanic trinity and exalt himself, above all that we humans call God.

Babylon on the Euphrates, and Mystery Babylon, the whore that sitteth upon many waters, will both be dealt with by God himself, one never to be inhabited again, and one relegated to the annals of religious history!

As Israel finally consolidates the land, and begins to build our Messiah's temple, the world around them will be looking to consolidate power under one government where the entire religious pagan pantheon will be accepted for a time. A treaty with Israel of some sort, will be ratified by the United Nations which by this time has moved its Roman Catholic and Muslim headquarters to Babylon and Baghdad.

After three and a half years, the satanic trinity will break the covenant and look to gather all the armies of the world who have flown the eagle, to battle, and they will gather in Assyria between the Tigris and Euphrates rivers. Where the carcasses lie, there the eagles shall be gathered.

The bride is in Heaven receiving her mansion, and her crowns, as she prepares to return with Messiah to destroy all the nations of the earth who ever tried to stop the plan of God of placing Jesus Christ on the throne of David for 1,000 years. In Jerusalem.

But take heart, you still have martyrdom at the hands of the satanic trinity, by which you will enter heaven at the end of the millennial reign of Messiah on Earth!

He was crucified upon a cross of wood, yet he created the hill upon which it stood.

He is alive forevermore, and he is returning for his virgin bride very soon.

John Burns, 6-5-2022.

Where Have We Gone

Whenever I begin to pen words, I pray for those words to only be from God. My God is the trinity found in Genesis 1:1. My God gave me an owner's manual, and warranty deed over my life before he brought Adam into existence. My God wrote time in advance. He calls this book, the Bible.

Sixty-six individual books, revealed to at least forty-two men, over 3,000 years, all saying one thing with every letter, every number, every part of speech, every metaphor, every story, conceived by the trinity before they brought the universe into existence. That universe is the product of thus says the Lord.

Elohim is the creation name of God found in Genesis 1. It denotes one all powerful, all knowing, all consuming, God, in three distinct characters, a Father, a Son, and their link to men the Holy Spirit. Our creator exists as God, Jesus Christ, and the Holy Spirit all the time.

The trinity was reunited as the God-man at Jesus Christ's baptism to fulfill all righteousness. When Messiah came up out of the water, the Father and Holy Spirit in the form of the dove, united to fulfill God's perfect will for humanity: the crucifixion of the creator by those he created to witness of his majesty on earth.

Thy throne oh God is a scepter of righteousness. This is how God identified Jesus Christ to the Hebrew priests? Why?

The priests had separated the divinity of Messiah from the humanity of Jesus Christ, to cling to their religious presuppositions. They had grown comfortable getting paid for the message of God, and their temple had become more important than spending time alone in prayer and meditation of God's precepts found in his word.

They had hijacked his message, and now they were profiting from what God had done in their lives. Jesus Christ overturned the money changers tables because they were selling the sacrifices to the very poorest who needed mercy and grace, yet instead the priests held on to ancestor worship, religious traditions, and allowed pagan practices to permeate their temple.

The tabernacle written about in our Old Testament, was the most important place to a Jew. Proper understanding of the temple, will clear up all questions about how God views buildings we call church.

When Moses received the design plans for the Ark of the covenant, included were the plans of God to allow the Jews to build a temple. But not before he went out of his way, to show them he does not dwell in houses made with human hands.

The Jews had been in Egypt in servitude for Abraham's unbelief for 400 years now. They had witnessed YHWH defeat the gods of Egypt through the plagues. The last being the sacrifice of the firstborn. God's plan of redemption had been polluted in Assyria and Egypt, and the Egyptians had deified their Pharaoh, his wife, and their offspring.

The death of Pharaoh's firstborn son, was God reclaiming how he alone intended to redeem humanity through the death of his son. We will meet Pharoah's son in Heaven for he was taken before the age of responsibility to God, which is twelve. God removed him before he brought the judgement and wrath of YHWH upon Pharoah, and Egypt, for treating his people so badly.

I spent the majority of my life, trapped in human religion. I was taught to do what my ancestors did. My first problem, was who exactly were my ancestors?

On my father's side, they were easy to discern. My Dad, was descended from Scotch-Irish Catholics. My grandparents had seven children, six boys and one girl. They raised their children as Roman Catholics while encouraging them to experience change occurring in America.

My Dad would marry my mother and have three children. My brother Sean Michael had died. My mother was addicted to methamphetamine and valium, my father had answered his draft notice and was in basic training, when my sister and I were found abandoned and brought into foster care.

My Dad would receive a hardship discharge and come home to get his children back. My mother, I would not meet until I was a Christian and mature. I was forty-nine the first time I would meet my biological mother. I pray for her to receive salvation every day.

I would confront the narrative I had been raised with, as I meandered through life and began to question every presupposition I had formed in my life. If I was ever to fulfill God's perfect will for my life, I could never return to the place of my nativity. The gods of my parents had to be replaced by the God of the entire Bible. God's mission, had to become my mission.

As a Ranger squad leader, I was required to be a master and teacher of the Ranger handbook. My mission from my commander was to get men ready for war. Every aspect of Ranger life, comes from the foundations learned in the pages of the Ranger handbook.

My greatest award ever received for being ready for war, and having men trained to replace me if injured or killed, was the reward in knowing every member of my weapons squad who survived Mogadishu, went on to serve in the GWOT. Seeing these heroes years later, is the greatest gift bestowed upon a Ranger leader who earned his combat scroll serving with men much better than I.

Life's greatest reward now revolves around getting these men under the blood of the Lamb. It will never happen in church. Church is not there when a believer enters the valley of Elah unprepared for spiritual warfare.

The Bible alone is a Ranger's spiritual two-edged sword, to vanquish all the enemies of God who stage an assault on our lives when we testify to saving faith in Christ. Our sword requires we master it as a weapon. We need both edges to wield Old Testament mercy and New Testament grace.

The sword of the Spirit is the word of God. Become a Berean Ranger and master the Bible as a spiritual weapon. Faith is your courage. Hope is your battle cry. Love through Jesus Christ is what a Ranger Christian should offer everyone we encounter.

He was crucified upon a cross of wood, yet he created the hill upon which it stood.

He is alive forevermore, and he is returning for his virgin bride very soon.

John Burns 6-7-2022.

GRACE

The Virtuous Woman

Tucked away in the Proverbs of Solomon, is an amazing allusion to the relationship desired by Jesus Christ toward his espoused virgin bride. Proverbs 31 begins with an introduction to a King I can find nowhere in Bible history. Another mysterious King like Melchizedek.

His Hebrew name seems to point to a conversation between Mary and Jesus Christ. King Lemuel has a name that must be unpacked in the Hebrew tongue to fully comprehend what is taking place. Imagine a mother talking with a son about how a king should act, and how he describes what a virtuous woman should be.

The name Lemuel in Hebrew begins with the letter Lamed. It is the English letter L. It is the shepherd's staff or shepherd's crook. It denotes God's two divine attributes of mercy and grace. The staff has two ends, one for correction and one for blessing. One for mercy and one for grace.

The second letter in our king's name is the Aleph. It is the first letter in the Hebrew alphabet. Both Hebrew and English share the distinction of having twenty-two characters. Hebrew is a guttural sound language so vowels are not present. Every Hebrew letter tells an individual story.

The aleph is an ox. Both as a beast of burden and an animal to be sacrificed. It happens to be the first letter in the God of creations name. Elohim begins with an aleph. Jesus Christ said I am the aleph and the tau. The beginning and the end. The first and the last. The alpha and the omega.

The third letter in the name of King Lemuel is the mem. It is described as the living water. It is the water of refreshing and the water of divine judgement found in Noah's saga. It also happens to appear in the creation name of God. Elohim ends with the living water of Jesus Christ our Hebrew messiah.

Following the mem is the yod. It begins the name of YHWH. The yod are the open hands of God. The open hand of correction, that always precedes the open hand of blessing. The right hand of mercy preceding the left hand of grace. The open hands of God, nailed to a cross, yet still offering one thief mercy, and another thief grace!

Another aleph follows the yod in the name of our King. It can never be overstated how important names are to God. Every Hebrew name can tell the story of a person's life and mission. God our creator is sovereign over the affairs of men. It seems Lemuel is a picture of the believers promise from King Jesus.

Undergirding the entire Bible narrative is a story conceived by a loving God, outside of how we humans experience time. God wrote history in advance. With a little Christian humility, a desire to fulfill God's perfect will for humanity, and a newfound desire to learn the heart and mind of God, a believer can change the world.

A marriage covenant between one man and one woman is the pattern upon which God wrote the story. In Genesis, we are introduced to our pattern, Adam and Eve. One created in the image of God, and one taken from the created man. The man to be the protector, provider, priest, prophet and progenitor of humanity. He is endowed with the Godly attribute of mercy.

The woman brought forth to be the glory of man. She was endowed with the Godly virtue of grace. Her soul purpose is to be a suitable helpmeet in child birth, child growth, and child teaching of God's pleasing perfect will for the family. She is to be revered and respected first by the father.

The first attack from Lucifer occurred in Genesis with Cain and Able. The first-fruits of Eve's womb. One son who understood God's single plan of redemption, including the sacrifice of an unblemished male lamb for his sins. Another son filled with jealousy and wrath after denying God the first ten percent of his increase.

Enter Seth. His name transliterated into English means appointed. Seth was always God's plan for redeeming mankind to himself. He would marry the daughter of Adam, to keep the Messianic bloodline protected. God had appointed Eve the son of promise in Seth.

The next attack came as men began to once again worship and call upon the name of God, during the life of Seth. Apparently, the mark of Cain brought the vengeance of the fallen angel Lucifer, as he instructed the fallen angel army to begin to have sexual relations with the daughters of men.

Genesis 6 explains the war going on between the seed of the serpent and the seed of the woman. Nothing has changed. Lucifer will do anything to stop men from accepting Jesus Christ as Messiah to include divorce, adultery, abortion, idol worship, and every other perversion of the marriage covenant of Genesis 2:24.

Jesus Christ was promised a reward and an inheritance from God the Father for enduring the cross. They are mutually inclusive and mutually exclusive. His reward was to receive a gentile bride taken from all the nations of the earth as the good news of Christ's resurrection was taken to the four corners of our earth.

Jesus Christ's bride was to be a virtuous virgin bride. King Lemuel is talking with his mother explaining what indeed is virtue and where does it come from. The purpose of a bride for a coming king is to rule and reign with him in his coming kingdom. It is the pattern of all human history.

Jesus Christ's coming kingdom requires his reward to be unblemished. He alone is God and he alone is to be worshipped. His virgin bride exhibits Godly virtue only when she submits to the correction and blessing of her King. You cannot have one without the other.

A virtuous woman and bride to be, must forgo the Roman gods permeating Christian churches. We must all examine our relationship to Jesus Christ only through the lens of the entire Bible message to truly understand the Levirite marriage paradigm upon which God is fulfilling every promise found in scripture.

God has sent the comforter into our fallen world to find his son a bride. She is to be washed in the blood of the Lamb, and her testimony of saving faith in Jesus Christ is her perpetual act of service to Messiah.

A virtuous woman and virgin bride to Messiah, will go ye into all the world and share the gospel of mercy and grace. Jesus Christ alone, offers all those who would believe.

Become a virtuous woman by reading the proverb of King Lemuel as he instructs all on how to become the espoused bride of Messiah whose dowry was paid on Calvary.

He was crucified upon a cross of wood, yet he created the hill upon which it stood.

He is alive forevermore, and he is returning for his virgin bride very soon.

John Burns 6-19-2022.

The Paradigm of Jehu

I am indebted to two Jewish rabbis for every revelation God has ever shown me.

First, Rabbi Yeshua. We western Christians call him Jesus Christ. He is the most misunderstood teacher in human history. Often quoted, yet never followed. He is the Messiah to our fallen world, yet we have clung to Roman religious traditions, rather than trust his entire revealed word.

He is the second person of the creation Godhead. Our entire universe was spoken into existence upon his word. He is the authority over creation. He established biblical patterns in the Old Testament, to point us to faith in the word becoming flesh and dwelling amongst us in the New Testament.

He came to the lost sheep of the nation of Israel. Religious traditions had blinded them to the truth that he was indeed the Lamb of God proclaimed by John the Baptist as the savior of the world. They had grown comfortable in wealth and military strength. Pride would be there undoing.

He is the subject of every letter in scripture. Of the abundance of the letter, it is written of me. He is the only child ever born who knew the day he would die. His entire ministry was one of mercy toward his relatives in the flesh.

His ministry began with a proclamation from Isaiah 61, The Spirit of the Lord God is upon me, because the Lord has anointed me to preach good tidings unto the meek: he hath sent me to bind up the brokenhearted, to proclaim liberty to the captives, to preach recovery of sight to the blind, and the opening of the prison to those that are bound.

He stopped short of revealing the acceptable year of the Lord. That would happen when he unveiled himself as God, and unveiled the true bride of Christ from within the body of Christ, in his letter revealed to John we call Revelation.

He gave us the beatitudes that begin with blessed are the meek, for they shall inherit the earth, and blessed are the merciful, for they shall be shown mercy. Jesus Christ's thoughts are never men's thoughts. How often do men have the choice to show mercy, yet they turn to judgement and shaming?

He called fishermen, carpenters, tax collectors, religious leaders, a prostitute, his family and his friends to take his message to the four corners of the earth. He knocked a pharisee off his religiously pious horse and blinded him, to teach him about total dependance upon God for salvation and ministry.

He was wounded for our transgressions, he was bruised for our iniquities, the chastisement of us was upon him, and by his stripes, we are healed.

A man acquainted with grief. Abandoned by his friends when he needed them most. Denied by his own brothers until after the resurrection. Denied three times by the fishermen he confided in most during his ministry.

He accepted his judgement without uttering a word in defense. He carried the cross up a lonely hill. Dumb like a lamb, he opened not his mouth as the executioners drove the nails home, and raised him upon the cross for all the world to see who we had crucified.

Yehoshua Ha Nazarite V. Melek Ha Jehudim. Jesus Christ of Nazareth, King of the Jews. As a Hebrew acrostic; YHWH. That is who we crucified.

The Jewish rabbi who came in the power of God to offer his unending mercy and unwavering grace. To receive an inheritance and a promised reward from God the creator and first person of the creation Godhead.

His reward is a virgin bride taken from all of the nations of the earth of those who would cry out for his mercy and accept the dowry he paid on Calvary as he settled the sin debt account of all humanity.

His inheritance is to receive the kingdom of David in Jerusalem at the end of the time of Jacob's trouble, as God chastens the nation he birthed in Egypt back into covenant relationship to his Messiah son, Jesus Christ.

He is my Messiah and he alone is the rabbi who called me home to covenant relationship with him as his virgin bride espoused to him for all eternity as I eagerly await his return to receive me unto himself in the clouds at the sound of the trumpet. Even so come Lord Jesus Christ.

The second rabbi is Johnathan Cahn. He is the Jewish rabbi who confirmed prophecy I had been studying for twenty plus years. His uncovering of the patterns in scripture as it relates to men currently occupying the White House, confirms that the God of the Hebrew Old Testament is sovereign over the affairs of men. Jehu is Americas Judge sent from God in the form of Donald Trump.

His sole purpose from God was to annihilate the bloodline of Ahab and Jezebel in their modern abhoration as Bill and Hillary Clinton. Their adopted son was Joram, who served at the house of the moon god. None other than Barak Obama.

Trump was called by God to usher in the worst period in American history as the purveyors of death, hell, and the grave are brought to judgement by a man called by God to end the gentile church age.

No President in modern American history had the courage to do what Trump attempted. God is not done with Trump as President. He brought courage and resolve back to American policy that actually lines up with what God is doing prophetically as he fulfills the pattern of Jehu from the book of second Kings.

It was Donald Trump who had the courage to enact what every president promised but never had the courage to admit, that Jerusalem is the eternal capitol of our risen Jewish

Messiah and soon God will establish Messiah's millennial kingdom from Jerusalem.

Christian preachers have denied 87% of scripture to the detriment of their congregations. They purvey in the heresy that somehow God has divorced his covenant nation, Israel. Turn to the teachings of two Jewish rabbis and learn the patterns God established the Bible upon in eternity past.

He was crucified upon a cross of wood, yet he created the hill upon which it stood.

He is alive forevermore, and he is returning for his virgin bride very soon.

In Christ service, John Burns 6-26-2022.

Iron Mixed with Clay

In the book of Daniel chapter 2, we are introduced to the religion of Babylon under the reign of King Nebuchadnezzar. He is having nightmares of a recurring type. He calls the diviners and soothsayers from throughout his realm and presents them with an ultimatum. Tell me the dream, interpret the dream, or be cut in pieces and have your land and houses turned into dunghills.

Daniel is amongst the Hebrew boys brought from Jerusalem to serve the king as Jewish slaves and advisors. He clings to the knowledge that one day God will restore Israel in the promised land as promised to Abraham. Then they will await the Lamb of God in the temple in Jerusalem.

If the wisemen of Babylon fail, Daniel will also be cut in pieces. The fate of the Hebrews as a people rests solely on the relationship between Daniel and YHWH. Daniel reveals that no man can do what Nebuchadnezzar has requested, however there is a God who reveals dreams.

Daniel reveals the dream and then proceeds to give Nebuchadnezzar a view from behind the veil of eternity. God reveals the times of the gentiles in advance. Beginning with Babylon and ending with the revived second iteration of the Roman empire.

God chooses to reveal history in advance. His method of interpretation is to use a statue of varying degrees of metal as it pertains to what men crave most, the love of money. Gold, Silver, Brass, Iron, and Iron mixed with clay.

At the time of this revelation in Babylon the world had already been introduced to two Satanic super kingdoms. Egypt and Assyria. God has used both empires to chasten Israel. But the Assyrians are specifically called by God, each time he chooses to correct Israel's thinking. Micah 5:2 reveals that one day soon, God will again use an Assyrian for his intentions for Israel.

Babylon is identified by Daniel as the head of gold. Gold has been the currency kings place their pictures on in both Egypt and Assyria, then continuing in Babylon under Nebuchadnezzar. Gold is the primary currency in which all trade and commerce occurs at the time of Daniel's prophecy. Gold is the currency accepted by the priests in Babylon for the purpose of interpreting dreams by viewing the stars.

Babylon would be replaced by Cyrus of Persia in Daniel chapter 5. The arms of silver are a reference to Cyrus uniting two competing empires under one ruler from Babylon. Cyrus is a cunning leader the son of Astyages the Mede whom Cyrus kills to gain the Medo-Persian empire.

When Cyrus enters Nabopolazzar's palace he is greeted by Daniel who has opened the scroll of Isaiah to read God's plan for king Cyrus, as revealed to Isaiah 120 years in advance. Isaiah describes exactly how Cyrus would take Babylon without a pitched battle.

In one of the greatest engineering feats in antiquity, Cyrus instructs his generals to divert the Euphrates River and they are able to cross in water that is knee high. The Babylonians do not even realize they have been conquered for three days.

Cyrus would rule Medo-Persia and allow for the mixing of the Persian pantheon with the Babylonian religion passed down from Nimrod, the world's first dictator. Cyrus would conquer Lydia and move the Babylonian religion to the shores of western Turkey in the capitol city of Sardis.

Cyrus established the Achaemenid Empire in Babylon as the Medo- Persian empire. It would last until Alexander defeated Darius Hystaspes at the battle of Gaugamela in 323 BC. Daniel reveals the Grecian Empire in the eleventh chapter of his prophecy.

Alexander's life is chronicled in the tongue of Aramaic and predicts with incredible accuracy the career of this great Greek general well in advance of the events occurring. Greece is the breastplate of brass identified by Daniel as God revealed it to him.

Alexander's Greek empire would survive until Rome conquered Egypt and eventually the Jews throw off the yoke of the Seleucid empire in 168 BC. This allows for the rise of Rome as the legs of iron. Rome is described as a voracious beast devouring everything in its path.

Rome would split into the eastern leg of Rome in Constantinople, and the western leg which has existed either in secular or religious form since the Romans made Ephesus the center of trade in the eastern leg of the vast Roman empire.

The currency that came to describe Rome was the vast iron weapons and the advancement of metallurgy as carbon could be tempered into Roman weapons. Those weapons would subdue the entire ancient world and place Rome squarely on a collision course with the God of creation.

Iron would be the means by which Rome would wage war for the next 2,000 years. The Parthian Empire would finally fall under Hadrian, and Rome would assert its influence over the entire world. Emperor Marcus Aurelius subdued Germania setting the stage for the European monarchies to vie for the title of revived Rome.

America became the envy of the world when it saved humanity from annihilation by Amalakites in Germany dead set on stopping the plans of God to place Jesus Christ on the throne of David in Jerusalem. Now Amalakites are in charge of our nation and God's plans for Israel are not their plans.

Rome has never been fully united. There have been many empires who claimed to be revived Rome but they have all atrophied and America will soon share their fate. The iron mixed with clay will never fully harden until the bride of Christ is removed as the clay. God is the potter and we are the clay.

Today's currency is graphene. It is a two-dimensional carbon element that is a byproduct of the mining and usage of coal to provide electricity to our world. It is used in the production of every circuit in every device we use to create a world dependent on computers and smart phones.

We are in the final days of the gentile church age. Daniel 2 is a veiled reference to world history in advance. We exist in the age of the church of Laodicea as prophesied by Messiah. It is the final church and it has nothing good said about it.

It is time for national revival in America. We must return to sound Bible instruction from both testaments of our Bible. Prophecy details our history well in advance. Mystery Babylon has been revealed here in America as the world prepares for the ill-fated battle in the middle east to stop Israel from building the millennial temple.

They intend to stop at nothing from allowing God to place Jesus Christ on the throne of King David in Jerusalem. Where the carcasses lie, there the eagles shall be gathered! Rome in every form, has flown the eagle as their banner.

He was crucified upon a cross of wood, yet he created the hill upon which it stood.

He is alive forevermore, and he is returning for his virgin bride very soon.

John Burns 6-26-2022.

A Man Raised to Know God

King Ahab has ascended to the throne in Samaria. The Northern Kingdom has hardened to all things dealing with the monotheistic God of Israel. They have set up two altars, in Dan and Bethel for the purpose of worshipping the golden calf.

The golden calf must be rightly understood from the lens of Bible and pagan religious history. The recently delivered Jews who left Egypt, hardened to the God of Israel not twelve days into the desert of Midian. They would wonder for forty years until God allowed everyone born in Egypt, to die.

The cult of Mithras was established by Nimrod in Babylon. Marduk became the principle pagan deity over the entire Babylonian pantheon. His statue was the head of an Ox or bull, and the body of a man.

He is the patron deity of Babylon, and the Egyptians developed their own cult venerating the bull as the creator god who gave us the sun and moon. The Israelites had been delivered from 400 years of servitude in a pagan nation, now they enraged the God who delivered them.

Why was God so angry? If you take the Hebrew name of God first mentioned in Genesis 1, the characters that make up his name tell a story. Hebrew is the language upon which God spoke creation into existence. It was the Hebrew tongue through which Nimrod consolidated sin!

All ancient languages borrow patterns from Hebrew. Egyptian hieroglyphics are no different. When we lose presuppositions about human history, the story of man and the gods we venerate can be rightly understood through the lens of the Bible.

God's creation name is Elohim. This is the English transliteration of the trinity over creation. It begins with the Hebrew character Aleph. The ox or burden bearer. The ox is both a beast that provides sustenance, and an animal to be sacrificed. Elisha was plowing a field with twelve oxen, as he was instructed to sacrifice them before he received Elijah's mantle.

This is the story of God. He is the ox who supplies all of our needs according to his riches in glory. The golden calf, mocks God's plan to become the Son of God and be sacrificed for the sins of humanity. The golden calf is an idol mocking the plan of redemption.

Before God delivered Israel from Egyptian bondage, he brought twelve plagues upon Egypt for refusing to release his people to return to Canaan and begin building the kingdom which will one day be ruled by Jesus Christ from Jerusalem.

Each plague dealt with a specific Egyptian god, being venerated by Jews in Egyptian bondage. God intended not only to teach Egypt a lesson, he also intended to remind the Jews that he is the power over creation and the affairs of men.

After allowing an angel to kill the firstborn male in every Egyptian home both man and animal, Egypt capitulated and let Israel prepare to leave. The Pharaoh would enrich the Jews with wealth before releasing them to their fate.

Three days into their desert journey the Egyptian army appeared in their rear. God would protect them with a supernatural cloud by day, and a pillar of flame and fire by night. Eventually a showdown between the deliverer God raised up in Moses, and the army of Egypt was in short order. Israel would never be tested in battle until Jericho. God would deliver them without their help.

Pharoah's army would perish in the Red Sea. Egypt has never fully recovered from the humiliation at the hands of the God of Israel. Israel would fail miserably at purging the land of Egypt from the minds of their people.

Enter the golden calf. Israel had been given the oracles of God passed down from Adam to Moses. They knew God would one day become the Son of God in the womb of a Jewish virgin, yet they set up an idol to the cult of Mithras that they knew while in Egypt.

They were saying we do not need God any more, we are out of Egypt and we are wealthy.

The worship of the bull has plagued men since God wrote his plan to redeem man in the stars of heaven. When viewed in their order of brightness, the twelve constellations we view in the night sky tell the story of mankind and the single plan of redemption from God our creator.

Egypt had the cult of Mithras that Greece adopted into its creation pantheon. Zeus was the bull who seduced Europa. A veiled reference to the cult of Mithras being venerated by European monarchies as they competed for supremacy over the affairs of men.

Mithras has always represented the worship of money and power. Today in America the cult of Mithras is being judged by God as I pen these words. Wall street has become the modern cult practice of men worshipping their own ability to create wealth apart from the idea of God.

At the time of King Ahab, Israel had set up two golden calves. One to venerate their monetary strength, and one to venerate their own military might. Ahab once knew God, now he allowed his pagan wife to take Israel farther and farther away from the worship of God as creator.

Ahab has a Hebrew name that must be rightly divided. Aleph, He and Bet. His name transliterates as sown of God the Father. For better or worse, God's permissive will is who allowed Ahab to gain the throne of the Northern Kingdom made up of ten breakaway tribes.

A man called for God's purposes who chooses to leave God behind once he marries Jezebel, the feminine leader of the oldest fertility cult in human history. This is the story of Bill and Hillary Clinton. God has raised up Jehu in Donald Trump to destroy the house of Ahab, Jezebel, and Joram.

It is they who have fought to murder babies in the sanctity of the womb of the woman. It is they who allowed for the unfettered immigration of Muslim moon worshippers. It is they who have moved the democratic party away from the knowledge of God, toward the worship of Babylonian cults.

God wins in the end. The supreme court has been led by God to strike down the forced financing of abortion by people who claim faith in God. The war between God and Lucifer has reached its crescendo in America.

We must repent or we will be totally abandoned by God, as he judges Mystery Babylon, the mother of harlots and abominations of the earth. The whore that sitteth upon many waters. My America, which has gone the way of Baalim, and listened to charlatan men who get paid for God's message which was purchased freely by Jesus Christ on Calvary.

He was crucified upon a cross of wood, yet he created the hill upon which it stood.

He is alive forevermore, and he is returning for his virgin bride very soon.

John Burns 6-26-2022.

The Days of Noah

Such as in the days of Noah, so shall the coming of the son of man be. These are the words of Jesus Christ echoed to the Jewish priests in Matthew 24. What are the days of Noah, and what was going on for God to bring a flood to destroy all living?

In Genesis 3, Adam and Eve are shown incredible mercy and grace. They have been deceived by Lucifer disguised as the serpent. He got them to question the authenticity of God's word. At the time, Adam enjoyed first person communication with our creator.

From Adam to Moses, men chosen by God, communed with the creator directly. They had his word straight from his lips. We have the written revealed word to draw courage and strength. What does the Bible reveal about God our creator?

Most importantly, he delights in making and keeping his promises. Genesis 3 introduces humanity to the God who intends to save humanity, through his own seed. The method of delivery, would be a virgin girl descended from King David and Adam.

The seed of the woman would eventually crush the head of the serpent, but for now the serpent would bruise his heel.

The war between Lucifer and God, was continued through the worship leaders God created to replace him. His rebellion in heaven had caused one third of the angels to rebel with him. Now God was instituting his plan to redeem the entire creation to himself.

Ten generations from Adam to Noah. Genesis 5 teaches us a whole lot about our Bible, and the Christ who wrote it in eternity past. Moses was given the Torah in God's love language, Hebrew. The names of these ten generations of men transliterate into God's plan of redemption.

Adam has a name in English which transliterates from Hebrew with a meaning of man. Adam means man.

Seth has a name in English which transliterates from Hebrew to English with a meaning of appointed. Seth means appointed.

Enos has a name in English which transliterates from Hebrew to English with a meaning of mortal. Enos means mortal.

Cainan has a name in English which transliterates from Hebrew to English with a meaning of sorrow. Cainan means sorrow.

Mahallel has a name in English which transliterates from Hebrew to English with a meaning of the blessed God. Mahallel means the blessed God.

Jared has a name in English which transliterates from Hebrew to English with a meaning of shall come down Jared means shall come down.

Enoch has a name in English which transliterates from Hebrew to English with a meaning of teaching. Enoch means teaching.

Methuselah has a name which transliterates from Hebrew to English with a meaning of his death brings. Methuselah means his death brings.

Lamech has a name which transliterates from Hebrew to English with a meaning of despair. Lamech means despair.

Noah has a name which transliterates from Hebrew to English with a meaning of comfort. Noah means comfort.

What happens when I write their English meanings from left to right without any other written dialogue? You determine if it is a coincidence, that Moses wrote the ten names of the first ten generations of man prior to the flood, that identifies God's entire plan of redemption?

Man appointed mortal sorrow the blessed God shall come down teaching his death brings despair comfort. Whose death brings despair comfort? The blessed God. Despair to the unbeliever and comfort for the believer. Our entire salvation rests upon the message that God intended to die to save us. Religion has perverted this timeless message.

Woven into the entire Bible message is a war between the seed of Lucifer, and the seed of God. We have a choice on who our Daddy will be. Problem is, we cannot have both. This is why the law, was given! To show man he could never keep it, and to teach us all the things we need saving from. None more than the space between our own ears.

We have power from God that Lucifer does not. Angels cannot be saved and they cannot receive the third person of the trinity to guide them. Only humans were created for the purpose of God teaching Lucifer that he alone is the creator worthy of human worship every minute of every day!

For the weapons we fight with are spiritual not carnal, for the pulling down of strongholds. Our war is against principalities and powers of the air. Spiritual wickedness in high places. We are pawns in God's battle plan. Wield the two-edged sword of the Bible, and Lucifer will flee!

Lucifer attacked God's plan through his bloodline. First Cain killed Abel. Seth replaced Abel and men began to return to worshipping God as creator again. Lucifer responded by telling his angel army to court and marry the daughters of men. He was trying to stop God's plan of using the Hebrew bloodline to save humanity.

Genesis 6 Begins with the narrative in the days of Noah. Moses is our first witness to authenticate, Jesus Christ is our second. Our story continues with the sons of God and the daughters of Adam. They are giving birth to the men of renown. The warrior caste of half human and half fallen angel DNA. The giants of antiquity.

This perversion of the human bloodline is why Noah was claimed perfect in his generation by God, and deemed righteous because he believed the word and plan of God. God could use Noah. His daughters and sons had no fallen angel DNA.

This is what Jesus Christ was teaching, that in the last days perversion of the marriage covenant in any fashion would lead to the fallen angels returning to court the daughters of men. Will born again believers recognize these men of renown? I am praying for our perverse nation. We are ripe for fallen angels to permeate our insanely oversexed and extremely perverse generation.

Even so come Lord Jesus Christ…

He was crucified upon a cross of wood, yet he created the hill upon which it stood.

He is alive forevermore and he is returning for his virgin bride very soon.

John Burns 7-21-2022.

Make Thee an Ark

At a time when all flesh had corrupted itself upon the earth, God raised up a deliverer. He with his wife, his three sons, and his sons' wives, would be saved for God's purposes. The Nephillim, their wives, and their offspring were the targets of God's wrath. A worldwide deluge would be the creator's teaching tool.

Sin in Noah is never mentioned in the Bible prior to the flood. He is judged by God as perfect and righteous in his generation. Every prominent prophet in both the Old and New Testaments mentions Noah. Why? Is the meaning of his name important to Christians today? Have you built an ark around your family that God can use to save humanity? Is your ark, the cross of Christ?

Noah was commanded to build this boat. He alone knew what God was up to. He would teach his sons how God intended to save humanity through the seed of a virgin woman. His classroom and teacher were none other than Enoch, Methuselah, and Lamech his father. They had learned God's plan of redemption by memorizing the twelve constellations of stars they encountered in the night sky.

Daniel, Job, and Noah are mentioned in scripture together in both testaments of the Bible. Is this an accident or is it a deliberate design by God to teach us the pattern of suffering men called by God endured to believe in his single perfect plan of redemption?

Daniel is God's man in Babylon. He would serve Nebuchadnezzar, Nabopollasser, Cyrus the Great and Darius the Mede as a Hebrew advisor to the Babylonian and subsequent Medo-Persian Kingdoms. He would be placed in charge of the pagan Babylonian priesthood know as the magi. It was a hereditary priesthood, that God inserted a Hebrew prophet as head.

Daniel would keep God front and center throughout his ministry. He had built an ark. His ark was faith in the knowledge that God was going to one day save his people and return them to Jerusalem. He knew God intended to save humanity through an unblemished male Lamb taken from the line of Adam, through Noah, Abraham, and King David.

Daniel was unwavering in his devotion to the plans of God for humanity. For his faithfulness, Daniel was given the most important prophecy in the Old Testament that today is bringing the descendants of Jacob into faith of our risen King and Messiah, our Lord Jesus Christ.

Daniel was given insight about the exact day Messiah would present himself to the lost sheep of Israel and the common people would accept him, while the priests denied him as the Lamb and future King of Israel. They were comfortable with Edomite Herod and Edomite Caiphas as priest. They did not need God's Priest and King. Daniel 9:27 coupled with Artaxerxes' command in the book of Nehemiah prove history was written in advance by God!

Jesus presented himself as Israel's Messiah and King on April 6, 32 AD of the Roman calendar. This was the 10th of Nisan on God's calendar. This is the presentation day, when lambs were inspected by the priests after being presented by the people. We call this event Palm Sunday.

14 Nisan would see the Passover seder meal celebrated by Messiah prior to his betrayal by Judas our traitor. Judas' ark was the silver he received for the message of the Gospel. That silver bought the potter's field, where gentile strangers visiting Jerusalem are buried if they happen to pass while visiting.

Job is our next hero. His book begins with a lesson on who controls Lucifer in chapter 1. Proving that God will allow those he loves to be chastened by the fallen angel cult, to get them to repent and return to worshipping him alone. Lucifer is commanded to attack Job in any means he just cannot kill him.

First thing that happens is Job loses his seven children and his wife. This is important for in the end Job receives a double portion blessing, ending up with a new younger wife and fourteen children. The reason is, Job never cursed God while going through his various trials. An amazing lesson for believers today.

Job endures and in chapter 38 his correction by God leads to his incredible blessing. God takes Job behind the veil of eternity revealing just what man has perverted in the plans of God. We are introduced to God's Mazzaroth, the twelve-star constellations God used to teach the Pre-flood people's how he intended to save humanity.

When viewed in their order of brightness, the story begins with a virgin human and it ends with a lion ruling and reigning over all of the nations of the earth, from God's eternal city on earth, Jerusalem. The book of Job is God placing his stamp upon creation as sole creator.

Noah builds the great ark and he is given the command to pitch it within and without. Why? This is only done when someone is preserving something forever. Could the narrative of global warming lead to God revealing Noah's ark in the mountains of Iran? I believe so. God desires humans believe his word and nothing should say God's word and Bible history is absolute, like the discovery of Noah's ark.

Noah has three sons with three wives who leave the ark and travel three different directions, but not before a curse is placed upon the descendants of Ham. Noah planting a vineyard and getting drunk was not his problem, it was his anger toward his firstborn son, and the curse he places on his heir to be the grandfather of Messiah that makes God continue to honor the curse upon Ham's descendants.

Shem would be the recipient of Ham giving up his birthright by performing the first homosexual act in recorded history. The descendants of Ham are still under the curse until they repent of their own transgressions and get under the blood of the Lamb. The cross ends all curses for those who truly believe in God's single plan of redemption.

He was crucified upon a cross of wood, yet he created the hill upon which it stood.

He is alive forevermore, and he is returning for his virgin bride very soon.

John Burns 7-21-2022.

Be Fruitful and Multiply

God's goal from the beginning in Eden has been to convince men to believe in his plan of redemption.

When Lucifer rebelled before our world was made, he convinced one third of the angelic host, to bow down and worship him. The first rebellion in history was led by the anointed cherub that covereth, created perfect in wisdom and beauty.

The word covereth has to do with his position as archangel in charge of the worship of God. Corruption comes hardest on those anointed to teach God's single plan of redemption. The plan revolves around men being created as the replacements for those angels that Lucifer lost eternally for God during his first rebellion.

Angels cannot reproduce. There are only male angels. This should settle it in every man's heart, the exalted position of a woman in God's plan of redemption.

Humans were created uniquely for the purpose of reproduction to provide God with replacement worshippers.

Any perversion or false posterity is taken as rebellion away from God.

Many people in history have taken oaths of chastity. They all violate God's command to be fruitful and multiply. I frankly do not trust men or women who deny God access to children, to be raised to worship and honor him. Train up a child in the way they should go and when they are old, they will not depart from it.

How can men or women who have never had children of their own, attain the empathy toward children and parent alike, required to train up that child? Voluntary humility never gets anywhere in the kingdom of our God. To make one a eunuch is a perversion of God's plan.

Genesis 2:24 is the beginning of the paradigm of marriage and how God views marriage between his creation. For this reason, shall a man leave his mother and father and cleave to the bosom of his wife and the two shall become one flesh.

We must confront how absolute this command is. It begins with a statement of a God with a single reason for having a man leave his mother and father. That reason is to cleave to the bosom of his wife. This statement has everything to do with human reproduction and a single purpose for it.

When we get to the book of Malachi God gives his reason for why he allows one man to marry one woman for life. And wherefore one. Because He was seeking a Godly seed. The single purpose for marriage in God's plan, is for humans to reproduce and provide God with worship leaders.

Marriage is the paradigm by which God framed his entire plan of redemption. If one can understand marriage from

God's point of view and learn the ancient Hebrew wedding, you can begin to really understand why God desires personal relationship to Messiah every day, over church for one hour maybe twice a week.

Our entire salvation rests upon God preserving a bloodline from Adam to Messiah, that has been under attack. It has not stopped or been averted. Satan has perverted God's plan for humanity so badly, he must return soon to judge America, or he will have to apologize to Sodom and Gomorrah.

There is no place I have traveled where the perversion of genesis 2:24 has taken place than in America. In fact, now my government that was founded upon Judeo-Christian principals handed down from the Puritans and Jews who arrived at Plymouth Rock, openly legislates using Christian and Jewish money to mock the plans and morality of God. The Church has been silent since our government removed our children's weapons to fight spiritual warfare in wickedly high places.

After the supreme court removed prayer from public school in 1962, and the Bible in 1963, the family unit began to crumble. Leading to unadulterated sex and the assault upon the morality of God during the turbulent 1960's. Would it not be nice if Christians took to the streets to protest the immorality now being forced upon our nation? A real pushback on the immorality of this polytheistic government.

Who is looked at as leaders in our world from a Christian perspective? The Pope, cardinals, bishops, priests all have their foundations in Babylon.

They begin their career as a deacon, they receive a black shirt, black pants with a white collar. Archaeology has revealed these are the vestments of the Babylonian priests under Pontifex Maximus at the time of Nimrod. The Pope is the modern cult leader and his hierarchy all wear the vestments of Babylonian priests.

They are not the only ones. Martin Luther failed to get rid of the Nicaolaitan cult leaders disguised as men of God. The reformation failed to return us to our Jewish roots, and today Babylonian priests lead unsuspecting believers in rituals begun by Nimrod and Semiramis.

There is one mediator between God and man, the Lord Jesus Christ. God does not enjoy any kind of church hierarchy that begins with a voluntary humility toward reproduction, and God's desire is to have children raised that love his Messiah and coming King.

The bloodline of Messiah has been under attack and Lucifer's time is short. He has planned this all-out assault on God's people and their morality for a long time. Today, homosexuality, transgenderism, divorce on demand, eunuch priests over God's people, and all kinds of alternate moralities are being forced on our society and our children which begins when we release them to teachers who do not share our belief systems.

The Bible ends with a warning to those who would add to or take away from any word contained in scripture. They would suffer the plagues contained within. Romans 1 plainly states what happens when an empire turns its back on him as lone creator, he turns us over to a reprobate mind, leading to all kinds of abominable practices focusing on human reproduction and human sexuality.

The end result, is that a nation is abandoned by God, and despotic leaders become their curse. Name your poison, I have not seen a leader try to return us to Godly morality. Donald Trump began to fulfill prophecy. Those opposed to Godly morality have united to stop God's plan of returning Trump to the White House, and eventually placing Jesus Christ on the throne of King David in Jerusalem forever.

No one on this phony January 6th committee is committed to God's plan of redemption, they all have too much blood on their hands.

He was crucified upon a cross of wood, yet he created the hill upon which it stood.

He is alive forevermore, and he is returning for his virgin bride very soon.

John Burns 7-21-2022.

From Ham to Nimrod

The flood of Noah ended and the ark came to rest in the Himalayan mountains, most probably in Iran. Noah commanded his three sons to be fruitful and multiply. He instructed them to go in different directions, and repopulate the earth to fulfill God's perfect, pleasing will for humanity.

Noah planted a vineyard. When the grapes ripened, he fermented the fruit and made wine. He drank the wine to the point that he passed out, apparently naked. Ham approaches, and decides to violate God's instructions on relations between humans. He performs the first homosexual act in human history.

This is very important to understand with what is going on today. Ham was the eldest son and the heir apparent to all the promises God gave Adam and his descendants as long as they adhered to the marriage covenant and the raising of Godly offspring.

Ham surrendered his birthright to be the grandfather of Messiah. This pattern would manifest many more times in history. It has manifested today, as humans deny the covenants God established forever!

Ham has a name that transliterates as ruddy red to black in color. Ham's descendants traveled into Africa, Egypt, Cainan, and the lands between Arabia and Mesopotamia. It is the Hamites who introduce our world to the worship of the fallen angels under Lucifer.

Great astrological monuments and temples were constructed in Egypt, and the Land of Cainan. The fallen angels demanded men to sacrifice their children upon fertility altars. In Babel, Nimrod set up ziggurats from where to view the heavens, and an altar at the top to sacrifice human offspring.

The Hamites were cursed by Noah, infuriating God, setting in motion the past 5,000 years of warfare between cults venerating fallen angels who convince men to worship the sun, the moon, and the twelve constellations of stars, placed in the heavens to teach us God's single plan of redemption.

Ham is told by God that his descendants would serve the younger brothers. Slavery was established by God, as a means for Ham to repent and return to God's covenants. God tried many times to redeem the offspring of Ham.

Today they enjoy the same victory over curses when they believe Jesus Christ died to pay their debt to God as creator. Nothing but the blood of the Lamb will release the descendants of Ham from their eternal curse levied by Noah, then honored by God.

Ham is the progenitor of the first world dictator. His name is Nimrod. His first title is mighty hunter before the Lord. It is Nimrod that gave us the foundations for all pagan societies. His idea of civilization and God's idea of civilized are diametrically opposed.

Nimrod established his kingdom centered between the Tigris and Euphrates rivers in Mesopotamia. It is Nimrod who established great temples venerating the creation, moving away from worship of God as creator. These temples centered first around the worship of the moon and its agricultural cycles.

This is very important to understand with the rise of Islam globally. The first god, venerated by Nimrod was titled, Sin. He is the moon god. Second was Moloch, the sun god. Finally, the Mazzaroth of Job 38 was polluted, and astrology was born. Fertility cults were established by Nimrod pointing to human reproduction as a product of the stars.

These cults are the foundation behind every sin committed by men, as they questioned the authenticity of the word of God. The fallen angels led men away from worship of God, and today they have convinced the church to venerate Nimrod at the feast of Saturnalia during the winter solstice.

The pagan feast was called Saturnalia. A veiled reference to the fact that Saturn is the star viewable in the morning during the celebration. Saturn is the perversion of a title of Jesus Christ perverted first by Lucifer and Nimrod.

The winter solstice occurs between the 21st and 25th of December. Nimrod claimed to be born as the son of the morning on December 25. He in turn would take a promiscuous woman already married to his greatest fighting general.

Her name is Semiramis. It is she who perverted God's plan to birth a savior through a Jewish virgin. Her adultery and pregnancy required she begin a pagan mythology. She claimed to be visited by Moloch, the creator of the sun, and he in turn supernaturally restored her virginity, and impregnated her with a son.

His name is Tammuz I. He was proclaimed to be the son of God. From this heresy, every pagan religion in history was born. As a descendant of Ham, this religion traveled to Egypt, as successive monarchies began to claim to be gods and goddesses. The male offspring of these alliances, were deified by men.

Semiramis was given the title of Queen of heaven. Nimrod was proclaimed to be the creator who gave us the gods. They are venerated today at Easter and Christmas all around our globe, and God will not allow this heresy in church to go unpunished.

Synecretism is the mixing of two belief systems to form a religious tradition. Nowhere on earth, has pagan religious tradition crept into Christian tabernacles, then in the America I love. The time for repentance and a return to the truths of the Old Testament is right now.

Many are called and few are chosen. Repent and return to the hard truths of the Bible or find yourself left behind at the rapture!

Love is why God called me to study the Bible for the past forty-three years. It is the greatest decision I have ever made.

I love humanity and God loves his creation. His desire is for all men to come to the knowledge of Jesus Christ. To achieve this, he needs believers to leave pagan churches and return to the words of our entire Bible.

Humility is where our story begins and ends. Return to the foot of the cross, and ask God for mercy for bringing damnable heresies into houses claimed to be dedicated to the God of Jesus Christ.

He was crucified upon a cross of wood, yet he created the hill upon which it stood.

He is alive forevermore, and he is returning for his virgin bride very soon.

John Burns 7-22-2022.

The Patience of Job

The Christian blessed hope is not heaven, heaven is guaranteed when you accept Jesus Christ by confessing with your mouth and believing in your heart that God raised him from the dead. Salvation was purchased and your dowry was paid. Your blessed hope is in Messiah returning to remove you prior to the coming tribulation.

The Christian guarantee of removal at the end of the gentile church age must be biblically unwound, to return us all to true blessed hope. This event has been labeled as the rapture. The Greek word first used in Genesis concerning the removal of Enoch prior to the flood, and our removal prior to the tribulation is the Harpazo meaning to remove instantaneously.

There were three people groups God dealt with concerning Noah's flood. Those removed prior to the flood. One person, Enoch, he is a picture of the true virgin bride of Jesus Christ. He is the model and pattern God used many times in scripture to teach us of our removal prior to the judgement coming upon our fallen world.

The second group is those preserved through the flood; Noah, his wife, his three sons, and their wives. Eight people saved from the wrath of our creator. They were preserved for keeping the Messianic bloodline intact. Noah's sons and daughters-in-laws had not perverted themselves with the fallen angels. God could use them to fulfill his pleasing perfect will for humanity.

The third group God dealt with were those who perverted God's marriage covenant. These were the fallen angels, and human daughters who had intercourse and subsequent dual DNA offspring with. Their children are the Nephillim. The giants of antiquity.

God destroyed the world that then was. Now God intended to use the offspring of Noah to repopulate our world. Lucifer wasted no time. Fallen angels now returned and had convinced men once again, to worship the shining one. Jesus Christ's bloodline was once again under attack.

The Bible pattern is one where Lucifer constantly attacked Jesus Christ's ancestors to stop the plans of God of placing Jesus Christ on the throne of David, forever in Jerusalem. Job was no different.

The book of Job begins with a conversation between God and Lucifer. God issues an order for him to attack Job, and he begins by killing his entire family. Why would God allow this to happen?

The most misunderstood attribute of God is sovereignty. He controls every aspect of human interaction. God uses men most often, who do not realize they are being used. Job was a pawn in the war between our Creator and Lucifer, the anointed cherub that covereth.

Read Isaiah 14 and Ezekiel 28, and you can begin to comprehend your role in establishing God's kingdom on earth. It is a future, literal kingdom of Jew and Gentile believers in Yeshua ha Messiah, our risen savior, the Lord Jesus Christ.

Lucifer kills Job's wife and seven children by collapsing his family home. The grief Job felt must have been overwhelming. Lucifer was not done with Job, and neither was God. Next came boils upon Job's skin. Sickness is the second tool of Lucifer. Thank God Jesus Christ's thirty-nine lashes can heal us from the thirty-nine diseases found in our world as a result of the curse.

The same Holy Spirit that raised Jesus Christ from the dead, is available to all who would believe and dedicate their life to knowing Jesus Christ from the words of our Bible. We have plenty of structures in America where men claim faith in Jesus Christ, how many of them have supernatural miracles occurring regularly?

I personally will not sit under the teaching of men who claim the Holy Spirit and miracles were reserved for the first century church. Why would God wait 3,000 years to reveal the mystery of the Holy Ghost indwelling every believer, only to remove him from Christian churches? Miracles of healing are a means by which God authenticates his will for humanity.

However, God only heals those willing to repent and return to his written word. God's perfect pleasing will, is for all men to come to the knowledge of Jesus Christ. If you are willing to be chastened by God, and dedicate your life to achieving God's perfect pleasing will, physical healing awaits. You must crucify pagan religious traditions before God can use you!

Job was God's pawn to prove his authority over Job's life. His patience is a teaching tool for every believer, patiently awaiting the return of our risen Messiah and bridegroom to receive us unto himself.

Jesus Christ warned us that in the last days there would be scoffers in church. Saying where is Jesus and why has he not returned? The rapture is not even being taught consistently, yet it holds our true blessed hope as believers.

God desires a willing bride for his Son and coming King. He has been searching the world for those rare believers willing to forgo religious traditions purported by men, claiming faith in Jesus Christ, to be completely chastened by every word of scripture.

To be the virgin bride, the crucifixion of Roman religious traditions must occur in your own life, or you will be found wanting when Jesus Christ is instructed by God, to go retrieve your bride promised before the world was spoken into existence.

Job was tempted by friends to forgo the belief in God's sovereignty over his life, and just die. This is how you know whether a person is a man of God or not. Men of God offer mercy and grace, never judgement! Beware of those who claim a monopoly over righteousness.

All have sinned and fall short of the glory of God. The Bible was written to every human being. It is up to you to allow yourself to be corrected by the Holy Ghost. It is not your job to judge sinners. It is our Job to introduce them to our Messiah. He alone, is able to judge individual sinners!

He was crucified upon a cross of wood, yet he created the hill upon which it stood.

He is alive forevermore, and he is returning for his virgin bride very soon.

John Burns 7-23-2022.

Job's Reward

In the book of Colossians, Paul treats as believer to a history lesson as to the identity of the Son of God. The Hebrew law of inheritance must be understood, if a believer is to rightly divide who was on the cross. To understand Jesus Christ as God, one must grasp what God says in the entire Bible.

Giving thanks unto the Father, which hath made us meet to be partakers of the inheritance of the saints in light. Who hath delivered us from the power of darkness, and hath translated us into the glorious kingdom of his dear Son. In whom we have redemption through his blood, even the forgiveness of sins. Who is the image of the invisible God, the firstborn of every creature, for by him were all things created, that are in heaven, and that are in earth, visible and invisible, whether they be thrones, or dominions, or principalities, or powers, all things were created by him, and for him and he is before all things, and by him all things consist.

Beware lest any man spoil you through vain philosophy and vain deceit, after the traditions of men, after the rudiments of the world, and not after Christ. For in him dwelleth all the fullness of the Godhead bodily.

Hebrews 1:8 But unto the Son (He saith): Thy throne oh God is a scepter of righteousness.

Was Job a righteous man, and why? Did Job receive salvation in Christ by believing God would one day become a Lamb sacrificed to pay his sin debt? Jesus Christ is the propitiation for sin. Yesterday, today, and tomorrow. Our creator became the Son of God, in the womb of a virgin Jewish girl, to die to pay the sin debt of all who would believe. To include Job.

The Book of Colossians reveals a truth lost to most of the Church. In their haste to learn Greek hermeneutics to interpret scripture, they have lost 87% of Bible literacy. They have become those who separate Jesus Christ's humanity as a Son, from his divinity as the creator.

The Colossian letter teaches us about Gnosticism. This is a class of men, educated at western seminary who married the world and brought Roman-Greek paganism into our houses of worship. You will know them by the effort they make to separate Jesus Christ from his Jewish inheritance promised by God.

The Colossian letter introduces us to the Christians of Laodicea. An interesting point, for Jesus Christ would reveal Laodicea to John in 95 AD, forty years after Paul received the revelation to exchange the Colossian letter with the Church of Laodicea. Proving, God wrote all human history in advance.

Until one understands that the Bible was conceived outside of how we humans experience time, there will be no power emanating from their churches. Revival will not reach church in America until they repent of their move away from sound Hebrew Bible instruction, taught by Jesus Christ in the Gospels, and Paul in his letters, and away from Greek Eugenics taught at most western seminaries for 1,900 years.

We are living in a time the Bible says more about than the time Jesus Christ walked the shores of Galilee, and the streets of Jerusalem. Study to show yourself approved, a workman rightly dividing the word of truth. The two-edged sword identified by Messiah in Revelation 2.

What was Job's reward? Chapter 38 is the most amazing science lesson in human history. It outlines how we receive all scientific information from the creator. God was proving to Job, that as our creator, Job should rest knowing he alone holds the creation in the palms of his hands!

God goes to the extreme measure of placing Job's head in a tornado? How far has God gone to get our attention, and will we recognize the men he has anointed to chasten us all back to belief in him as creator?

We learn many things about what God created and how it all points to Messiah suspended between Heaven and Earth for the forgiveness of our sins as humans created in his image.

Job is introduced to the Mazza Roth. To understand this phenomenon, is to unlock everything wrong with church in America. Travel with me to ancient Egypt, to a pagan temple for our clue.

The Temple of Dendera is the oldest pagan temple on Earth. Inside the temple are tile mosaics on the floor. The greatest being the Mazza Roth. It depicts the twelve-star constellations common to all who could view the night sky.

This is why, we are all without excuse. God wrote the story of redemption in the stars. Beginning with a virgin, ending with a lion receiving a kingdom. When the stars are unpacked according to their order of brightness, they tell how God has always intended to save mankind.

The God who laid out the heavens and named every star by Jesus Christ, loves the creation, and he delights in making and keeping his promises from the beginning. His greatest promise was to become a Lamb slain, that would one day inherit his earthly kingdom, and after all our unbelief, sit down to rule his kingdom from Jerusalem. Hallelujah!

Proverbs 30 introduces us to the creator who holds the weather, the wind, the storms, and the entire creation, in the palms of his hands. Do you realize these are the same hands that were nailed to the cross of Calvary?

How many Christians understand how far our creator went to redeem the creation from the curse?

How many Christians understand Jesus Christ as creator?

Revival will begin in America, when God and his Bible are placed back in the hands of our children and the science of creation is once again taught in public education. Trust our children to decide whether God indeed went this far to prove he loves his creation.

He was crucified upon a cross of wood, yet he created the hill upon which it stood.

He is alive forevermore, and he is returning for his virgin bride very soon.

John Burns 7-23-2022.

Jeremiah 10

Hear ye the word, which the Lord speaketh unto you, oh house of Israel. Thus, saith the Lord, learn not the way of the heathen, and be not dismayed at the signs of heaven: for the HEATHEN are dismayed at them.

For the customs of the people are vain: for one cutteth a tree out of the forest, the work of the hands of the workman, with the axe.

They deck it with silver and gold; they fasten it with nails and with hammers, that it moves not.

Sounds like Christmas to me! What is it about the celebration of Saturnalia, that caused God to warn ancient Israel to not do like the heathens do? Why is Christmas vain, and will God pardon professing believers for perverting his plan to redeem man, and replacing salvation with Babylonian pagan traditions.

I am the Lord your God, you shall have no other gods before me. Yet Christians venerate Nimrod, whom men referred as the god who created the sun, moon, and stars. He is the first in a long line of pagans who claimed to be born on the winter solstice. Around the 25th of the pagan calendar month of December.

Why does this infuriate God our creator?

We have followed a delusion for a long time. The Church married the Roman pantheon of gods in a pagan temple town known as Pergamos. Jesus Christ refers to this town as the seat of Satan on earth, and he labeled it one of his churches. This should alarm people.

Yet, church folk continue to deny 87% of the Bible to their own peril. Will God pardon professing believers who are doing exactly what he punished Israel for? I think not. He that has ears, let him hear what the Spirit is saying to the churches.

You shall not covet thy neighbor's wife. How many preachers have been married multiple times? I am guilty. I need the blood of the Lamb covering my frailties. Thank God Jesus Christ is saving me!

You shall not covet thy neighbor's goods. Yet Christians turn their children into jealous beggars during every holiday venerated by men. No one is content. Everyone wants what others have, even though Jesus Christ says do not store up for yourself treasures on earth, where moth and rust decay, store up for yourselves treasures in heaven. This is an allusion to Christian testimony and winning souls.

God views treasure as a soul plucked out of the fire and placed under the blood of His Lamb.

It is better to celebrate the day of one's death, more than the day of one's birth, Ecclesiastes 7:1. Only pagans celebrate the day they are born, our God celebrates the day you are born again.

Jesus Christ never celebrated his birthday for he would violate his own word. He celebrated the day he would ascend Calvary and be sacrificed for the sins of humanity.

If Jesus Christ did celebrate his birthday, he would celebrate on the first new moon of spring in the Hebrew month of Nisan, when lambs bound for the temple sacrifice are born every year in Bethlehem. It has never changed. The lambs are still born every year in spring, and only in Bethlehem.

Babylon is the city at odds with the God of creation eternally. Mystery Babylon is the mother of harlots, and abominations of the earth, and will be destroyed by God, for allowing polytheism to inhabit the places we claim to worship God in. Babylon gave us the feast of Saturnalia.

Saturn is the planet visible to the naked eye in December during the winter solstice. It is also the place where fallen angels claim Lucifer controls creation from. He is assigned the title son of the morning in Isaiah 14. A veiled reference to the holiday that pagans, venerate his birthday. Are we mocking Jesus Christ?

The mistletoe. A Babylonian aphrodisiac. Another gift of Nimrod and Semiramis. A game played by two perverse rebels. It was placed above the doorposts in homes. It held mystical powers of reproduction. When two people walked under the mistletoe, Nimrod or Semiramis could make them perform sexual intercourse between the sexes. Even between the same sexes!

The Yule logs. The Chaldean word Yule is transliterated into English as an infant. Israel was warned to stop throwing their offspring onto superheated fertility altars brought into Cainan by the fallen angels.

Jesus Christ warned 1st century Christians from consuming food sacrificed to idols. Have we lost sight of what angers God? Why have we condemned our children to a life of vanity and covetousness? I pray for our nation, as the abandonment wrath of God grips the America I love. Our feast days all venerate Lucifer, not Jesus Christ!

This is the hard truth. My suggestion is repent of the easy lies of church tradition, and get under the blood of the Lamb, if it is not too late. Martyrdom awaits those who do not change! God will not compromise with any pagan tradition that violates his Word! He has exalted his word above his name!

How did we get here? Humans seem to always take the easy road. It is easier to attend church and never question authority. The path of least resistance has led to Lucifer having a foothold in our houses of worship. The fruit of these practices has led to the manifestation of the delusion God had warned us was coming.

Christmas, Easter, birthdays, Mother's Day Father's Day, and Valentine's Day are all compromises Lucifer has introduced to church, and Christians are being led to the slaughter! It is time to make Jesus Christ Lord over our lives and it begins when we open our Bibles every day to find out if what I am saying is true, if the rapture has not already occurred?

I am a devout monarchist who believes in a coming kingdom ruled by Jesus Christ from Jerusalem. My plea for mercy resonates every day. I pray for true revival in America and it begins by placing God back in our homes and the removal of every idol worshipping Satan Clause and his minions who have led our children away from biblical monotheism.

He was crucified upon a cross of wood, yet he created the hill upon which it stood.

He is alive forevermore, and he is returning for his virgin bride very soon.

John Burns 7-24-2022.

You Who Killed the Prophets

When writing becoming Jezebel, I prayed often for the courage to teach what Christians need to hear. They get want they want to hear, every week in church.

The Bible is the most misunderstood book of anything ever written. I completely understand now, why Jesus Christ warned the Ephesian Apostolic church, that they had lost their first Love. Spending two hours in church twice a week, had become more important than giving God their time.

Educated men in the model of the pharisees, opened religious houses of learning, where their interpretation techniques were being taught. Their individual belief systems, influenced what men and women learn in church. They advanced an outward piety model.

After King David had Uriah killed, and he had impregnated his wife in an adulterous relationship, the high priest and the prophets wanted David punished openly by God. David reminded them, the God he serves does not judge by outward appearance, but by inward conviction.

He realized the part of him that God desired to save, was not his flesh, for his spirit and soul were sanctified by God, and God alone was able to judge David righteously. David quipped; I do not care what men think, for I serve the living God!

Imagine if Christians had the courage to never worry about what other Christian gossips say? Imagine if Christians returned to thus says the Lord in both testaments of the Bible? Christianity would again become the light of the world!

The Bible teaches us the purpose for why the trinity gave us the word of God, before our universe was spoken into existence. All scripture is God-breathed, for reproof and correction. Every heresy being purported upon believers and unbelievers, Jesus Christ saw coming. The Bible alone can correct an individual believer.

The New Testament can be rightly understood, only by grasping the Old Testament. The New Testament is concealed in the Old Testament. The Old Testament is revealed in the New Testament. For every scripture pointing to the first coming of Jesus Christ, there are at least seven times as many pointing to our soon return of the bridegroom to retrieve his bride. Our God wrote every day of human history in advance.

What is missing from Christian houses of worship is hard truth. Most Christians have become completely comfortable never questioning the doctrines of their ancestors. This has led to Lutheran Christians and Roman Catholics rationalizing the killing of Jews during World War II.

Antisemitism gripped the first century churches and it has now continued for 2,000 years and counting. Greek, pagan hermeneutics replaced sound Hebrew interpretation techniques employed by every writer in the New Testament.

Men began to build great three-dimensional churches looking just like the pagan world around them. The first century church endured persecution, and people met in the houses of their friends. God is once again saving people in the homes of their friends with no need for buildings where people practice syncretism.

The Gospel is being lived in the sinful world again. People who are searching for a Messiah, are finding him in common people not caught in Roman religious bondage. No need for churches God is not in. His desire is to inhabit the tabernacle of the human condition, one believer at a time.

Go ye into all the world and preach the Gospel. Last time I checked, there were more people not in church than there are people in church. God desires sinners to be saved. How can that happen if people in church never bring Jesus Christ to the world around them?

It is as if a hostage crisis has been going on. The kidnapping of God's plan in buildings God says he is not in, for he does not dwell in houses made with human hands. Christians have gotten comfortable believing in a form of God, while denying the power of God, to the majority of humanity.

The Church married the world in Pergamos under Constantine. Pagan practices were welcomed into Christian worship, and now our children have been turned into covetous beggars around every holiday venerated by professing believers. Repent Christian America, for our time is short!

God has turned his attention east toward Jerusalem again. Jews are coming to Jesus Christ all over the promised land. Israel is in their land and prospering. This is a reference to the end of the gentile church age. The rapture is on our near horizon as the virgin bride of Christ.

Christianity was never going to be the majority opinion. Men were always going to move away from sound Bible teachings in favor of monetary comfort. There is no middle class in Christianity. We all are poor in spirit if we weep over what made Jesus Christ weep.

For what are those wounds in thy hands? Those with which I was wounded in the house of my friends.

Not only was Messiah crucified, but after his resurrection his disciples denied the resurrection until they could physically touch him? They had lost their first love!

Have we become doubting Thomas's and deny the supernatural power of the Holy Spirit in our lives, available to all those who would believe? I yearn for miracles of healing, and resurrection power emanating from churches again. I doubt they will have the humility to listen to the prophets they would rather euthanize in favor of continuing in pagan bondage.

God has raised up men willing to forgo the trappings of wealth and power once again, in favor of winning souls for Jesus Christ's coming kingdom. The Shmita will manifest in September 2022 and the American economy will collapse.

What will churches do then? I pray they will return to, thus says the Lord before the majority of professing believers are left behind at the rapture.

Repent and return to a personal relationship to Messiah and become the virgin bride of Christ eagerly awaiting the return of our risen Messiah, Jesus Christ.

He was crucified upon a cross of wood, yet he created the hill upon which it stood.

He is alive forevermore, and he is returning for his virgin bride very soon.

John Burns 8-01-2022.

Special Operations Wounded Warriors

2016 was my official homecoming. The community I once served, was asking me to serve once more, but not before welcoming me home.

It had been twenty-three years since I returned from Mogadishu, Somalia injured. It had been a long time since I had toasted the men I lost, and brothers I never got to say goodbye to. This organization exists to find men like me. Brothers-in-arms who somehow got lost on the road after doing exactly what their creed requires. Somewhere along the way I had stopped Rangering. Or so I thought.

I was a United States Army Airborne Ranger. I spent five years in a Rifle Company in the 75th Ranger Regiment. I would dare to say the best Ranger rifle company the Regiment has ever seen. I was one bearing in the gears of Bravo Company that when in time, made the whole engine work. Bravo Company was home to me, and the men I served with are my family. The DNA that makes up our family, can never be manipulated. It is a blood covenant.

Rangers serve at the behest of the president. They are as close to tier one as any unit gets. While not always enjoying the budgets of other special operations units, no unit has been asked to do more for our country. And Bravo Company has led the way every time.

On Rio Hata in Panama, Bravo Company 3/75 lost SSG. Larry Bernard and Pfc. Roy Brown, with Bill Dunham and Patrick Kilgallen suffering injuries that still remind them each day of their sacrifice. These men are the reason I served.

I had the privilege of welcoming these men home from the hospital in 1990. I have remained a steadfast advocate for my brothers and my best friend in life served in their platoon in Panama. Paul Mercer is the greatest Ranger and best American I have ever met and called my friend.

I remained In B 3/75 for five years. I served in positions ranging from Mortar Section FDC Chief, Team Leader in a Rifle Platoon, Squad Leader of a Rifle Squad and culminating in my job in Somalia, Weapons Squad Leader, Third Platoon B 3/75 Rgr Regt. The greatest privilege the Lord Jesus Christ ever bestowed upon me was the privilege to lead Rangers in combat. Nothing since has kept my attention.

In Somalia I had an amazing group of men in my squad. My three machine gunners were all better than me at being a daily Ranger. Dominic Pilla, Chris Schlief, and Dave Ritchie are three amazing Americans. Dominic would die in Somalia leading with lead, and killing his killer. Chris Schlief was unwavering in Mogadishu, and the most brilliant man I have ever encountered. He has continued to serve our country in special operations and today he is A CSM in an SF Group. Dave Ritchie was my gunner on my vehicle on October 3, 1993. He is my hero. He was wounded early in the mission and continued to fight with an M16 after his Mg was disabled. Dave ended up leading our vehicle home when I was wounded near the front of the convoy for the third time. Dave was a Spec4 in Somalia. I had my gunner Clay Othic wounded seriously with the loss of his shooting arm. Lorenzo Ruiz took over the 50 caliber, and was fatally wounded taking over from Clay Othic. I was wounded once by gunfire early, and once by Shrapnel before I was hit the third time making my way back through the convoy toward my vehicle. That left a Spec4 in charge of my vehicle team, and the rear of the convoy. Dave Ritchie was able to lead them for two hours as we fought our way back to our base. Dave Ritchie would go on to serve in Task Force 160th as a CH 47 pilot for every year of the GWOT. He retired a CW4, and continues to serve his state as a pilot fighting forest fires in California. He is an American Special Operations hero.

Chad Fowles was an AG for Dave Ritchie and drove our vehicle. He somehow managed to not get hit in Somalia. God has a plan for Chad Fowles, and I pray SOWW helps him find it. Chad retired as a MSG with twenty years in the Army. Along for the ride on my vehicle was PFC Jason Dancy. He also managed to not get hit, but it does not diminish his contribution to the Regiment and Bravo Company lure. He fought like a Spartan on October 3, 1993. Reese Teakell was Chris Schlief's new ammo bearer in Somalia. His first deployment in Bravo Company was to Somalia. Reese went on to serve the Regiment after returning from Somalia in every position from team leader to squad leader to CSM of the Special Troops Battalion. He is today a CSM in a Brigade of the 82d Airborne division. Ed Kallman rounds out weapons Squad who fought on October 3, 1993. He was the driver for another vehicle and managed to not get wounded. I was privileged to lead these men in support of the Special Operations mission to Somalia. I intend to work tirelessly to bring these men home to SOWW and back together as a Ranger family.

I left the Army in 1995. I was a Platoon Sergeant in Vicenza, Italy. A final act of mercy from a loving God. I got to share with my platoon in Italy the lives of my squad, and their heroism in service to the Regiment and SOCCOM. I live every day for the chance to share my life and it's struggles with my Ranger brothers and SOWW is the platform that continues to make it possible.

As the country debates our nation's path forward, one thing that is undebatable. The true 1% of Americans that should be recognized are the 1% of Americans that have actually volunteered to defend the American life we enjoy on battlefields most Americans know not exist. When you break it down further, less than 1 tenth of 1% of those ever serve in a special mission unit. The freedom we all profess comes at a cost that continues to be paid for by the 1 tenth of 1% of Americans who get to call themselves the SOCCOM family. It is a family that can never be divided, and SOWW is the greatest mechanism for keeping the family recognized and together, as we embark on the next phase of our lives.

America has once again become apathetic to all things military. We can never surrender. If we surrender, this entire experiment of a government of the people, for the people, and by the people will perish from the earth.

SOWW exists to make sure America never forgets the lives led by Rangers, Seals, Operators, and Airmen, who continue to provide America with a blanket of protection. The freedom we enjoy is because of men who serve in SOCCOM. SOWW is the place where SOCCOM family reunions continue to occur.

I was privileged to meet a man I now can identify as my brother while attending a SOWW event in South Carolina. I was stepping out in extreme faith by attending this event. My Ranger brother, and survivor of Mogadishu, Dave Floyd had invited me to the annual SOWW hog hunt called Takin Bacon. I accepted and boy was God a gracious God. Not only did I connect with men I had served with, I got to meet an entire generation of special men who had now served our country in a protracted war with no end in sight. But one I will never forget. Eddie Oglesby was one of the dog handlers. I felt there was something more to Eddie so I struck up a conversation with him. Eddie had served our nation in Viet Nam as a Ranger in Papa Company 75th Infantry. He and I were DNA brothers, and we were meeting at SOWW. I sensed Eddie was experiencing his own sort of homecoming. SOWW was the mechanism by which Eddie and I connected, and we will be brothers who look forward to Takin Bacon every year. I miss Eddie every day. He taught me more about responsibility to my brothers than any shrink could ever hope to learn in twenty years of practice. SOWW did that for me and an old Ranger from Viet Nam who came home to a divided nation. Imagine the Rangers coming home now?

SOWW provides special men with the opportunity to share their experiences with people who will be able to show empathy rather than sympathy. The stories would never be understood by a public that has lost its sense of understanding toward freedom's high cost. Special Operations Wounded Warriors caters to the needs of men who have been wounded defending our ideals as Judeo-Christian Americans. Our creeds are our bond and promise to this nation. Our experiences in war are our bond to each other.

SOWW has put its money where its mouth is. Warriors from the SOCCOM community gather each year in March to fellowship, kill wild boar, and party like it's 1999. The place where this occurs cost money every year to lease. We at SOWW have been afforded the opportunity to purchase the property and make it a permanent destination throughout the year for men and families in our very small community who have borne the brunt of this protracted war on terror. It will never end, and our mission to our community will never end. Consider giving a monetary gift to further our mission from once a year to permanent status. The property along the river comes at a cost of three million dollars.

I know the Ranger community alone could raise that! This organization is limiting the damage to warriors in our community who need us to continue the family bonds on into eternity. We have borne the brunt of the freedom debt our country expects us to continue to pay. Please help us reach our goal.

Donations to our cause should be sent via www.sowwcharity.com.

Please prayerfully consider helping our cause. It is our nations cause!

RLTW John Burns, He was crucified upon a Cross of wood yet he created the hill upon which it stood 6-9-2020.

A portion of the proceeds from the sale of every book will be donated to Special Operations Wounded Warriors in the name of Daniel D. Busch.

A portion of the proceeds will also go to Behind the Veil Ministries in the name of CW2 Aaron A. Weaver. My Ranger brother, an American hero, and a friend to all things Jesus Christ.

The rest of the proceeds will support Gold Star programs supported by the USSOCCOM community. We owe these family members continued support as they navigate this life without the brothers we served with.

Rangers lead the way!

Biography

John Burns is a staff writer at the Morgan County Today newspaper, the Chaplain of Special Operations Wounded Warriors non-profit, and the President of Behind the Veil Ministries Inc.

His Christian faith is the foundation for every aspect of his life. He is married to Susan C. Burns of Lancing, TN. He is blessed with four grown children; Sean, Andrew, Kasey, and Lisa. He also has eleven wonderful grandchildren.

His hobbies include; turkey hunting, hound dogs, hog hunting, beer tasting, coffee drinking, and studying the Bible every day.

His ministry to the special operations community was born out of his desire to serve the community that gave him so much in life.

"The men who came before me were giants. They led the way and ensured we would give it one hell of a go. I have so many to thank. The only way I know how is to serve them tirelessly so we can all fellowship forever on the other side of glory."

The road goes on forever, and the party never ends…

He was crucified upon a cross of wood yet he created the hill upon which it stood.

Printed in Great Britain
by Amazon